Unbearable Splendor

Also by Sun Yung Shin

Rough, and Savage
Skirt Full of Black

Unbearable Splendor

Sun Yung Shin

COFFEE HOUSE PRESS
Minneapolis
2016

Coffee House Press books are available to the trade through our primary distributor, Consortium Book Sales & Distribution, cbsd.com or (800) 283-3572. For personal orders, catalogs, or other information, write to info@coffeehousepress.org.

Coffee House Press is a nonprofit literary publishing house. Support from private foundations, corporate giving programs, government programs, and generous individuals helps make the publication of our books possible. We gratefully acknowledge their support in detail in the back of this book.

Library of Congress Cataloging-in-Publication Data
Names: Shin, Sun Yung, author.
Title: Unbearable splendor / Sun Yung Shin.
Description: Minneapolis : Coffee House Press, 2016.
Identifiers: LCCN 2016010964 | ISBN 9781566894517
Subjects: | BISAC: LITERARY COLLECTIONS / Essays. |
    POETRY / Ancient, Classical & Medieval. | POETRY / Asian. |
    FAMILY & RELATIONSHIPS / Adoption & Fostering.
Classification: LCC PS3619.H575 A6 2016 | DDC 811/.6—dc23
LC record available at https://lccn.loc.gov/2016010964

Printed in the United States of America
24 23 22 21 20 19 18 17   3 4 5 6 7 8 9 10

The cyborg is resolutely committed to partiality, irony, intimacy, and perversity. It is oppositional, utopian, and completely without innocence. . . . Unlike the hopes of Frankenstein's monster, the cyborg does not expect its father to save it through a restoration of the garden. . . . The cyborg would not recognize the Garden of Eden; it is not made of mud and cannot dream of returning to dust. . . . The main trouble with cyborgs, of course, is that they are the illegitimate offspring.

—Donna Haraway, "A Cyborg Manifesto"

I've seen things you people wouldn't believe.

—Roy Batty, Nexus-6 Replicant, *Blade Runner*

Unbearable Splendor

Valley, Uncanny

Don't let the name fool you: a black hole is anything but empty space.
—NASA's website, Astrophysics page, Focus Areas, Black Holes

Where's the hole's end?
—김혜순 Kim Hyesoon, "A Hole"

A valley makes a kind of hole. A hole open on two sides. Korea—an island on three sides. South Korea—an island: water, water, water, DMZ. North Korea—water, water, DMZ, the People's Republic of China.

I was a hole and I brought it, myself, to 미국 *mi guk* "beautiful country," America, the United States. I carried a train of holes—holes of smoke, holes of sky. Holes of water, holes of rice milk. I was an uncanny guest. Two years old. A week after arrival from Korea, a brother, born in America, asked, "When is she going back?" Like the heavenly maiden with too many children to carry, too many holes to go back *t(w)here.*

There is a limit to canniness, but not to *being* uncanny—it is infinite, 무한, *mu han.*

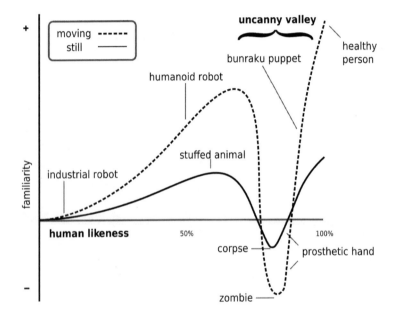

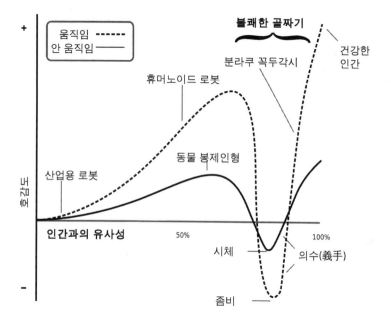

To many immigrants, exiles, and pseudo-exiles, *back* becomes a manifold; space and time—an asymmetrical nonevent. *A hole surrounded by light that pours in and down like Niagara Falls. In my boat is my nameless two-year-old self and my nameless adult self. We approach the water; the air around us glitters. When my past self reaches out to touch the rushing white wall, like a dress she is wearing, I mimic her gesture . . .*

Maybe I am a kind of star. Burning—sending you light to read by. A valley you might come upon gradually, not a hole to fall into.

When are we all going back? There is no *back,* there is no *there* there. Like the travel of light, upon arrival, the star may be dead. Time can be fragile. It can be a blossom, and when you peel away the petals, that hard, dark face remains.

"Most famously, black holes were predicted by Einstein's theory of general relativity, which showed that when a massive star dies, it leaves behind a small, dense remnant core."[1]

I lost my name and I stepped onto this corner, this half frame, the axis. It was empty in that moment. White space, cousin to the black hole. I had my face, my feet, my duration in time.

---

1. This quotation and those that follow in this section are from NASA Science, "Black Holes," accessed February 19, 2016, http://science.nasa.gov/astrophysics /focus-areas/black-holes.

One small step onto vertical Y and horizontal X, at the crossroads between *familiarity* and *human likeness.* I could keep walking into this space, eating this time, and drawing it into me like thread through the hole of a needle. I could stitch it to me.

The positive rising into infinity—an arrow on which *familiarity* travels without limits. Rope to heaven. Fraying, frayed.

The negative descending not into infinity but into dusk, oblivion, the nihilism of Freud's *unheimlich.* We have always known, we humans, about holes.

"Although the term [black hole] was not coined until 1967 by Princeton physicist John Wheeler, the idea of *an object in space so massive and dense that light could not escape it* has been around for centuries."

The opposite of *what is familiar* is *infinite possibilities of startling encounters.*

One after another, after another.

How much of one's life can one spend on the approach?

There is not always a name for what is [*unheimlich*].

Two lines, each like one train track, travel through space—to plunge into the valley.

     moving _

     still _____

My performance of childhood rode both rails. This machine of love. This language machine. This hole made for survival. The hole was like a shadow that changed at will. The spaces between *moving* and *still* widened and narrowed and rushed and plunged and lazed like a river.

Act natural, act natural.

> My father built a robot,
> a creature of industry,
> a tool with a perfect face and perfect thoughts.
> A memory made of magnets.
> I crawled into its inner space.
> My memories, now holes,
> pooling above each temple.
> My mother gave me a creature,
> a toy, a "stuffed animal,"
> one without a motor but with a string I could pull
> to hear its voice
> over and over again.
> It was not difference, but repetition.
> It could not dance or sing, but it could travel.
> It could fall lightly into holes.

Others who pass too close to me may be subject to certain processes.

"If a black hole passes through a cloud of interstellar matter, for example, it will draw matter inward in a process known as accretion. A similar process can occur if a normal star passes close to a black hole. In this case, the black hole can tear the star apart as it pulls it toward itself."

Two gorgeous words: *toward*   *itself*

*   *   *

My dreams are the ivory gates, the bone gates, the accordion, a mouth, a mind, that same floret splitting away from its hard, dark face. Some bulbs are good for eating, some are good for sleeping, repairing, emitting time like a bomb. Radium.

Sometimes there are horns or hooves waiting to be fitted to my head and hands, feet. A tail swishing away the space-dust of any remaining light.

In my dreams I passed before the axis of human likeness, a black line that had to be contained on all sides, a pipeline.

> A kind of dark traffic.
> Men in uniform were posted all along its length.
> Some had cameras, some had guns.
> To slip down its invisible curtains.
> Like sheets tied together and hung out of a hotel window.

Underneath, the *ur*-world, without measure or mark. Here I communed with each at its station:

Corpse

> Zombie

> > Bunraku puppet

> > > Prosthetic hand

Not holes but **force**. Electricity, instinct, momentum, the vigor of our "lives"—so many words for a progression, like chords, sine waves, lines:

Contract
Heaven
Paradise
Human (Likeness)

     Moment
     Lapse
     Error
     Mistake

          Incident
          Accident
          Event
          Episode

               Emergency
               Crisis
               Disaster
               Catastrophe

                    Dystopia
                    Apocalypse
                    Time
                    Expand

There is a code for every kind of duration. One must be careful to carry the right holes on one's journey. Forth. Back. X. Y. *Toward the familiar . . .*

The bottom of the valley is the palm of time.

There, one finds rest.

All objects fall at the same rate.

No outside, no inside.

I spent sixteen years living with American parents.

They are inside me now, they are my guests.

They are my holes, like babies, like stones.

I have a thousand valleys inside me.

Descent upon descent.

The swallowed becomes the swallower.

Egg, star, event, time, hole, black, bound, devour, collapse.

Reaching for—

"However, as the star collapses, a strange thing occurs. As the surface of the star nears an imaginary surface called the 'event horizon,' time on the star slows relative to the time kept by observers far away. When the surface reaches the event horizon, time stands still, and the star can collapse no more—it is a frozen collapsing object."

There   i   s   n   o   e   n   d

When I'm at home
people don't ask me who I am
They know at once that it's me
because I'm the only one who's home
and so all kinds of things enter me.
—김혜순 Kim Hyesoon, "Shadow Janitor"

The Hospitality of Strangers

OLD ENGLISH *GÆST, GIEST* (ANGLIAN *GEST*) "GUEST; ENEMY;
STRANGER," THE COMMON NOTION BEING "STRANGER,"

Consider all doors.

Opening of an ampoule, space, wind > light.

Animal its sere, stiff robe, canters in place, species against every epoch, flower-skull and the last kick far between. Velocity capillaried like water ringing a tree.

Still-limber, hunt-cut, child-bundled. Dark star and diurnal wash all the same soaking in.

Or doored as the boards of the ship that sent you. The vessel that brought you, the arms that pulled you. Vessel, your queer coffin, your name following your overboard.

All the shipwrecks sailing within us. I must disembark at every coast inside me. The docks grow open as mouths.

FROM PROTO-GERMANIC **GASTIZ*
(COGNATES: OLD FRISIAN *JEST,* DUTCH *GAST,* GERMAN *GAST,*
GOTHIC *GASTS* "GUEST," ORIGINALLY "STRANGER"),

FROM PROTO-INDO-EUROPEAN ROOT *GHOS-TI-
"STRANGER, GUEST; HOST" (COGNATES: LATIN HOSTIS
"ENEMY," HOSPES "HOST,"

Hospital. Shelter for the needy.

Metal doors and bars. Tragic panthers inside for your own protection. Head down, animal. Acquaint the glossy side of your face with the cement floor. No competition here, no culling. You're the last one. You're the last sterile one.

Under bridges, cardboard castle, trash moat, hate moat. No meds no job no home. Something in your blood is bad. Your brain is in your blood. Drain, salvage, hide, blind.

Eight billion pine boxes today! Long-stemmed roses in a box from Mexico for everyone. There isn't not room for everyone. Who was here first. Private property the work of God. Discipline and disobedience. My blank body: dim root with a thousand eyes. Splitting into the dark. They finger their way down. Eat dirt, spit dirt, be dirt.

But your body doused with oil; the wrong side of the ground, a sister digging a grave in the air.

Your body all in flames—*witch, bleach, blanch, stitch, torch, clutch.*

Library of bodies borrowed. Returned. Scholars to the last.

Strange deck of cards, pages in gorgeous disarray, the last book written.

Amnesty.

FROM *HOSTI-POTIS "HOST, GUEST," ORIGINALLY "LORD OF
STRANGERS;" GREEK XENOS "GUEST, HOST, STRANGER;"

OLD CHURCH SLAVONIC *GOSTI* "GUEST, FRIEND,"
GOSPODI "LORD, MASTER");

Waiting for white rope, become the unbraid. Raveled, ends burned closed, heavy as hair. One day we will all be sea.

Does my day stalk me or do I grow it within me. My first and final masterpiece. Breath, brush, breath, bath, last.

My enemy, my house, my horse, my hound.

Border, brother, bastard. Every eye a sorrow meter, every ear a room of private silence. Clouds of it. Storms moving through.

Feast, fast, guest, host.

Every room of this life; all of us guarding the wrong things.

One country of the living. This port.

> Dickinson dared you to see a Soul at the White Heat.
> Then, let us crouch within the door.

THE ROOT SENSE, ACCORDING TO WATKINS,
PROBABLY IS "SOMEONE WITH WHOM ONE HAS
RECIPROCAL DUTIES OF HOSPITALITY,"

REPRESENTING "A MUTUAL EXCHANGE RELATIONSHIP
HIGHLY IMPORTANT TO ANCIENT INDO-EUROPEAN SOCIETY."

Bend your good eyes toward the crashing ceiling of water. Ever-changing door. You can't open it. You are already in it. It is home and tomb. Womb and veil. Wall and wail.

A guest here. My dowry everywhere.
Come to the races. Lucky number. A thousand trousseaux . . .

Flag, gown, and shroud.
Loomed and unloomed. A woman with time in her hands. Bedded, unwedded. Inventory possessions: father, son, missing husband, servants, loom, bed made from an olive tree, drunk suitors, money, land, some beauty . . .

Magnetic field of the earth, yield your bombs. Spit them out. Regrow the limbs. Identification papers back in the jacket. Tanks reversed, tracking backward. Children tucked back into their beds.

BUT AS STRANGERS ARE POTENTIAL ENEMIES AS WELL AS
GUESTS, THE WORD HAS A FORKED PATH.

One Hundred Days in the Cave

> The person looking for a fixed identity is often the same person
> looking for God (escape into emptiness).
> —Fanny Howe, *The Winter Sun*

This empty (escape) room burns my (fixed) bonds.

*

According to radiocarbon dating, humans have been present on the Korean peninsula since about 40,000 BCE. It seems that art, or decoration at least, did not exist until 4,000 BCE when the inhabitants of the peninsula began making pottery with comb patterns scraped or scratched into the clay before it hardened.

Clans were absorbed into other clans. Fishing, farming, and hunting.

The introduction of metal from the Han civilization brought with it improved farming and an ability to make visible social hierarchies through the production of symbols of power such as dolmens (burial chambers).

And also through the production of more effective weapons.

*

Earl of Wind, Master of Rain, and Master of Clouds.
The Bear and the Tiger.
These were worshipped by the natives before being replaced by sun worship.

Metal equaled power.
Bronze daggers, iron mirrors.
Other forms of reverence were smashed and swept away.
With the Bronze Age came the Koreans' foundation myth and, with it, a justification of theocracy.

*

Koreans, according to their creation myth, are descended from a male god and a female bear.

> Korea's only indigenous religion is Shamanism, [which] is connected to the beliefs of tribes in Siberia. Shamanism is the belief that everything in nature has a spirit. The human world and the spirit world must be in harmony. A shaman has the ability to communicate with the spirit world.

> According to the [creation] myth, Tan-gun [the grandson of the King of Heaven and a bear-transformed-into-a-woman] founded Choson [known as Korea in English] in 2333 BCE. Interestingly, historians also use that date as the beginning of the nation. However, the first people to settle in the Korean peninsula were probably from the Ural Altaic region.

> Archaeologists have discovered artifacts in Korea that reflect the beliefs of Siberian Shamanism. Numerous golden crowns that have been found in Asian tombs have artistic motifs like those worn by shamans. For example, Tan-gun was born under a birch tree. Some tribes in Siberia believe that the birch tree is like the sacred World Tree in Norse mythology. The marriage of Tan-gun's parents may be interpreted as the union of two different tribes that ultimately create a new kingdom. Tan-gun's father's heavenly origin contrasts with his mother's ancestry as

bear. David A. Mason, author of *Spirit of the Mountains,* thinks this may be understood as a Heaven-worshipping tribe (invaders from Siberia?) absorbing a less-developed bear totem tribe (in ancient Manchuria).[2]

I feel myself from a young age to be all bear, no god.

*

Some beginnings. Seoul, South Korea. Spring 1975.
The baby has stridor. Notes are made in thin black script on charts. Nurses bow, bend, take the bus home.

The baby exhibits abnormal breathing with a high-pitched sound, the neck and face swollen, blue lips, blue nail beds, bluish skin.

The medical records look like a musical score of the body: its excretions, its color, the temperature of the interior.

We have inside us a series of red rooms, lesser and slighter, minor and more secret.

Paper soaked in milk.

Made itself sick.

The stethoscope, its metal methodical ear cupped to the hot and hollow places of the body— sounding the depths.

2. The Korea Society, "Exploring Korea's Creation Myth," accessed February 19, 2016, http://www.koreasociety.org/index2.php?option=com_docman&task=doc_view&gid=144.

Long poem as prescription. The doctor is memory. Thick as a rib.
Skin-paper.
Blood is water and iron. A million motes of oxygen. Bind, bound.
Slippery remembrance. Punishment and sentence.
Penance.
Absolute apology.
Absolute forgiveness.

The Other Asterion, or,
The Minotaur's Sacrifice (A Story)

The English word *disaster* is a combination of *dis* (bad)
and *astron* (star). *Bad star.* An event caused by an unfavorable
alignment of the sky-bodies. A *calamity.*

But of all the games, I prefer the one about the other Asterion.
I pretend that he comes to visit me and that I show him my house.
With great obeisance I say to him "Now we shall return to the first inter-
section" or "Now we shall come out into another courtyard" or "I knew
you would like the drain" or "Now you will see a pool that was filled
with sand" or "You will soon see how the cellar branches out."
Sometimes I make a mistake and the two of us laugh heartily.
—Jorge Luis Borges, "The House of Asterion"

"It's a remarkable piece of apparatus," said the officer to the
explorer and surveyed with a certain air of admiration the apparatus
which was after all quite familiar to him.
—Franz Kafka, "In the Penal Colony"

Prologue: The Cosmos Births the Prisoner
An empty symphony of velocity. In the beginning of the world there
was nothing. If you listened very closely, with your ear tilted toward
the void, you could hear it breathing like a great silent bellows, and
all you could hear was the sound of nothing expanding and nothing
contracting. The invisible lungs of the universe. No color and noth-
ing to see or taste with. Within the breath coiled something like a
tensed muscle, something readying itself to spring. Patient as a tro-
phied hunter or a benevolent mother.

After a nearly infinite number of years of this unhurried inhala-
tion and exhalation, a scintilla of dust entered nothing.

Nothing swallowed this particle and a mote-sized convul-
sion, a miniscule choking, an imperceptible gagging on this speck,

this impurity, this idea. Like a proto-Jonah it was engulfed but not digested, swam inside the vast nil, blinded by its darkness. Its inner absence. It became an untouchable inner navel within the black hole. That pinprick of mental noise deep within a quiet mind. A bit of grit inside the oyster of the protocosmos. The first queen of the first beehive, her perfect hormone-weather waking the drones and workers into sensibility.

Some might say that this was the origin of our conscience. What might grow into a moral reckoning. The itch of guilt or the deeper burn of shame. A pebble dropped into the deep end of the pool.

A tremendous force began bending the nothing within itself, a spring or a bow being drawn inward further and further, tighter and tighter to the point of breaking. When the bow was as thin as nothing itself, when the strap was as thin as sound, there was a great release. And from this violent freeing of energy hurtled a billion pieces of light with a thick protective halo of space around each of them.

Each dense portion of space unfurled and expanded like a lustrous flower opening toward the sun. Something opaque and endless thinned a nearly imperceptible amount. Somewhere else, a sheet of darkness began cracking, moving inward from its unseeable edges.

Eventually, through a series of violent clashes, Earth was born and glistened blue and green, and life began its cycles of formation, competition, adaptation, evolution, and extinction. There was and there shall be no escape from this great wheel, this inescapable machine. The land choked with lava, hot then hard. The evolution of the eye. Fearsome creatures from nightmares and dreams.

Unfathomable oceans of ice scraped their way across the surface of the planet, trapping and grinding everything to frozen dust and carving out vast scars and bowls.

Handprints on the walls of caves and spears sharpened. Primates walking upright. What we call hominids. *Afarensis, africanus, habilis, erectus,* and others. Axes. Necklaces and earrings.

Theft. Abandonment. The first murder.

Gods invented, feared, and prayed to. Sacrifices of all kinds. Animals roped and yoked. Virginity named and fetishized. Priestesses. The first kings and queens. Altars and the first permanent structures built. Architects and slaves. Grave goods buried with their illustrious owners for use in the unending afterworld. Copper, bronze, iron, silver, gold. Sword and shield. Horses and soldiers. Money and its malcontents. Seductions and infidelities.

The idea of crime. The invention of the criminal. Banishment and exiles. Other punishments to the mind and body.

Architects and inventors.

Churches and temples and altars.

Mazes and labyrinths.

The first prison.

Prisoners.

*

*   *

Part One: Asterion and a Peculiar Apparatus
I am a guard at an unusual prison. In fact, it is the only prison in the world, or the universe, for that matter. Actually, I will admit to you, reader, that this prison is indeed the universe itself. But it has many tricks and uncanny ways, and one of them is that it is a real prison on the real planet and houses real people, who, the moment they enter the prison under guard and their cells under lock and key, become something other than people. They become prisoners, they are defined by the structure that keeps them within it. Many metaphors may come to mind: a baby within its mother, a snail within its shell, a hand within its glove, a corpse within its coffin.

Like music captured and trapped in a parallel, one-dimensional world of black lateral ovals (some empty, some filled in) and vertical lines on lined paper, the prison comes alive when it is expressed through the actions of its prisoners. The prisoners, in this way, are like musicians in an orchestra. There are an infinite number of them, and there is an infinite combination of notes that can be played. Yes, these sounds are purely imaginary, but they are nevertheless an endless game of high elegance.

Our time is recursive and forking. Our time is a garden in which all realities are simultaneously possible. All paths are truly one path. From the time of birth to the time of death, every word you utter is part of one long sentence. This sentence is utterly, heartbreakingly unique. Never before and never again. Yet they, in ensemble, create One Sentence. It holds and houses us. Announces and defends us. Blesses and confesses us. Curses and condemns.

As I tend to them, the prisoners, I must pay attention to and interact with the physical structure; I don't know if I am more like an instrument tuner or a minor conductor. An orchestra may not be the most fitting analogy, but it allows me to think of my vocation as somewhat elegant, rarefied, with the potential for beauty, if even the beauty has a hint of violence, like a piece from the romantic period that evokes emotions both sublime and savage.

At the orphanage where I spent my formative years, nearly everything a child might need was scarce, except for music. Of this there was no shortage. One of the nurses loved music and had a phonograph that was kept in the atrium. The music—all kinds—filled the dark rooms and hallways and even the attics and porches like water. The long dormitory in which I slept and kept my few possessions was, while a long way off from the atrium, able to receive the sound as if it was flowing right to me, enveloping me, entering me. After coming of age and leaving the orphanage, I continued to seek that same auditory experience—hearing as if underwater, or hearing as if music was life itself—but have yet to find it.

Now, in the prison, I have to do without real music. I am more like an ear, or a machine that records live music, as I am always present to listen to the prisoners and the sounds of the prison as it interacts with them. If only I could play every moment back infinitely and relive each moment, broken into segments of my own choosing. But it doesn't work like that.

I tend to the prisoners. I say "*I* tend to them" because, it may surprise you to know, I am the only guard. In fact I am currently the only person at the prison aside from the prisoners. There is no warden, no physician, no librarian, no cook, no janitor, no shop teacher, no psychiatrist, no chaplain, no teachers, no lawyers, and no visitors—so far.

I confess that I harbor a longing for music and part of me keeps a small portion of hope alive, like a tiny flame in a glass jar, that someone or something will arrive with music. No one here can sing and no instruments are allowed. So I go on, waiting. If there is an end to my obligation here, my first step will be to find a record shop and I will search for the music through which I floated every night as a child.

Sometimes I dream that I almost hear it, that it is hovering somewhere nearby, but morning breaks the spell and my day begins, like in the vacuum of space, without sound. Sound cannot exist without something through which to move, and perhaps the air here is too thin, too evasive. If I close my eyes and put my hands out in front of me, I can feel the air eddy around me, swirling and silent.

Every nine years I have a special duty. It involves the receipt of a gift. Some call it a sacrifice. *Surrender, give up, suffer to be lost.* We can choose to look at this transaction in a variety of ways. Some say that these nine people, these nine young men, are guilty. They must be cleansed.

This duty is directly related to my favorite prisoner, or, really, my only prisoner. He is multiple prisoners, he is one prisoner. He has the ability of bilocation. He can be in two places at once. He can be in several places at once. He wears time like others wear clothing. Space folds and unfolds like an origami bird.

This year, the youths arrive, as usual, on time. They appear in the space outside of the prison, as if dropped there by the hand of a god.

I would say *they arrived on the doorstep,* but there are no doors. There are no windows. There are no bars, no locks, no keys. No stairs, no ceilings.

Asterion, on these occasions, waits in the center of the prison. His house. He is sometimes eager to show the youths around this impossible compound. He reads books on philosophy, books on various types of propositions, possible and impossible. Books of logic and the real and the unreal. The actual and the fictional.

Though he has the head of a bull, no flies worry Asterion about the face and ears. This is fortunate because unlike whole bulls, he has no long tail with which to swish away irritations. He has hands, beautifully formed, and a thickly muscled neck holding up his strong, velvet-furred head. The rest of his body is also nobly made, and white as marble or mother's milk. He has no need of clothes. Or weapons.

I greet the youths at the entrance. One is crying silently, tears trickling down his smooth cheek. Others show fear on their faces. Still others have a distant look. One begins singing a folk song as I lead them through one of the many passages. Once a person reaches the inner section of the labyrinth, there is no return. The way back is impossible without guidance. None have escaped. Asterion has long ceased looking for an exit. Oh, the first many months there was so much anguish, always walking the halls and paths, keeping the flame of hope kindled. Each week he spent fewer hours wandering the identical passages. Rubbing his beautifully colored horns against the hard walls, even to the point of breaking them. At last he accepted his fate. He is the master of his house.

The nine youths are drawn inexorably toward the center. Though the labyrinth is flat, we are like water running downstream and there is no possible reversal. Gravity itself is drawing the nine to their shared destiny. In this, together, they have a fortune denied Asterion. Asterion, the only creature of his kind. His mother's love could not save him, just as the youths' mothers' love cannot rescue them.

I have led this ritual so many times I have lost count. The youths, though surely individuals, have come to take on a cast of sameness to me. Straight hair, curly hair. Tall, short, wild-eyed, dull-eyed. They may be individuals when they enter, but like separate raindrops pitching into the wide, iron-colored sea, they merge as they fall.

Eventually, after what sometimes seems like infinity, we arrive at the central area of this special structure. Here I leave them, not needing to bear witness to what is shortly to follow. The nine huddle together, backs touching backs, limbs shuddering, waiting. As I walk away, I hear Asterion's steady, light footsteps coming closer.

*

*   *

Part Two: The Favorite Games of Asterion
After, there is never a trace of them. The youths have, for my purposes, disappeared. There are no mass graves, no burial mounds, no mausoleums, no tombstones, no grave markers. No bodies. No bones. No clothing. No sandals. No dirges.

What remains is a slight iron scent and a very sluggish prisoner. His eyes unfocused, his gait uneven, and his speech slurred, he must be helped to bed. This I do gladly. His body is almost unbearably hot to the touch, as though an inner furnace is operating at full capacity, but he himself always shivers. It's as if he feels all the cold in the world. As if he is not surrounded by air but by great banks of snow and ice.

He allows me to lay him on his bed. With his great and fierce head resting on his pillow, a thick blanket pulled up to his chin, he always sleeps for some time after the disappearance of the youths. Sometimes it's hours, other times days. Often, after I leave him, I turn back before reaching a bend and regard him. With all but his face under the bedding, he could almost be a real bull, whole and complete. *If only his true father, the snow-white bull, could see him now,* I think to myself.

It is during these times that I find him in other rooms of the labyrinth. Though I am but one, he is many. In one chamber he is arranging flowers in a white vase. In another he is swimming, attempting with great effort to keep his heavy head above water, resting frequently at the side of the pool, his great round eyes looking toward the sky. In yet another he is pretending to walk up the nonexistent stairs and admonishes me to *hurry, hurry or you'll miss the marvelous concert on the second floor.*

As I see it as my duty to provide comfort to the prisoner, I play along. I say, "Will the famous so-and-so be playing first chair?" or "Shall we pick more flowers tomorrow out in the fields beyond the palace?" or "Your father's servant says that dinner is almost ready and he is most eager to have you join him in his private dining hall."

This last one is a variation on one of his favorite games, or little plays. For like a play, it is something real and something unreal, all at the same time.

Sometimes I play his father, the king, and at other times he does. Sometimes I play his mother, and other times he wants to. One time, during an especially long period of sleep, the chamber bloomed with Asterions, each making its own courtly gestures, pantomiming conversations with imaginary guests. Even dancing, bowing, pretending to eat on plates with forks and knives, as humans do.

In my off-hours, when I am sleeping, not nearly so deeply or as long as my prisoner, but deeply enough to dream, I see a parade of youths passing by me. Each looks into my eyes with the saddest expression you could imagine. Each says, "I want to live. I have just begun. I want to walk through to my future. I want to master a trade, marry, have children of my own. I want to grow old and feel the sun on my face in my own courtyard. Help me." And to each one I must turn away. Sometimes I wake, my pillow wet with tears. Whether they are tears of the youths or my own, it is impossible to tell.

After a period of Asterion's high spirits and theatrics, he often falls into a deep depression. It is indeed like he is in a deep hole, so deep he does not even think to call out. During these times, I cannot rouse him from the floor of his bedchamber. He does not groom, his room gathers dust because he will not allow me in it with a broom and mop, and he seems to age years in a few weeks. The skin around his eyes turns a deep color and his eyes lose their luster. His pearly horns fall off.

Nothing cheers him up except, occasionally, stories about his beloved sister Ariadne. Before he came to his house, he and Ariadne played throughout the palace. She did not fear him or scorn him, as others did.

She tied ribbons around his horns and played hide-and-seek. Her laughter was like flowers. She told him the stories of their family, how their oldest brother Androgeus traveled to Athens to take part in their games. He won several of them and, out of jealousy, was murdered. Ariadne told Asterion that their mother had said that Minos was never the same after the death of Androgeus. Ariadne declared to Asterion that he, Asterion her baby brother, was her favorite. She would say with the seriousness of a child, "Asterion, I could never love anyone as well as you!" Though their other siblings cursed him and insulted him, calling him "Monster!" "Bastard!" "Abomination!" they didn't dare when Ariadne was near.

Asterion mostly ignored the insults of others, secure in Ariadne's affection and protection. Because no tutor would go near him for fear of his accursed condition infecting them with misfortune, Ariadne took it upon herself to teach him his letters, sums, the laws of the natural world, the names of the star formations in the sky, poetry, song, and dance. Rules of the court. Military history. Everything a prince would need to know.

Though she was but a child, Ariadne was skilled at many crafts, especially weaving. When Asterion was born, she began a tapestry containing the story of his life. As he became older and wilder, the tapestry became more graphic, disturbing. After his birth, mirrors were outlawed in the palace, and Asterion looked to the tapestry to see how he appeared as he grew.

I wonder if Ariadne has kept up my tapestry, Asterion has mused wistfully since then. *I'm sure she has, and I'm sure it is a thing of unrivaled wonder,* I have replied. He has, at those times, drifted into unspoken reveries. Sometimes I have hummed, tunelessly, until he has fallen into a light, peaceful sleep.

*

*   *

Part Three: Like a Band of Iron
Nearly nine years passed in relative tranquility in the house of Asterion. I went about my business as usual. There were always a thousand things to do. Adjustments, repairs, improvements, maintenance. Busy as the town's carpenter, or a housewife with her many children.

Time wheeled forward, and it could be felt as a kind of vibration throughout the prison. An almost tangible force. Sometimes thick and other times paper-thin.

As usual, though the world turned, neither Asterion nor I felt the ravages of time. Had there been mirrors, their serene surfaces would have shown no advancement of age, or only momentarily, and then erased, reverted. And though I did all the work while Asterion lounged like a nobleman, fatigue never visited my limbs, and weariness remained a stranger.

And before I knew it, the week of the nine was almost upon us.

Always before, I was my own person. I had my role to fulfill, yes, but I chose the order and manner of my duties. I had a great deal of latitude in running the prison and caring for my ward. I was comfortable with my routines, though I felt the edges of a craving—a craving for music from elsewhere—begin to stir within me, somewhat stronger than usual. I didn't dare to hope that it meant that my time here was almost at an end. I was not prepared for what was to come.

Mysterious changes arrived—starting with me.

Seven days before the expected arrival of the nine, I began to feel a slight headache, from which I had never suffered before. *Healthy as a horse,* Asterion always used to say brightly. *Knock on wood,* I would respond with equal cheer. I drank more water and tried to close my eyes when the sun seemed too intense. I gritted my teeth and tried to ignore the incessant pounding, a throbbing so regular it seemed to overshadow and mock the beating of my heart, the pulsing of my blood.

Six days before the arrival of the nine, my own fingers and feet went numb as blocks of stone. They even looked pale, as though the blood were retreating from them, slowly, like a tide receding with the moon. It was difficult to carry out my tasks as I tried to compensate for the lack of sensory perception. And the headache did not subside, but grew solid and rigid, like a band of iron around my skull.

Five days before the ceremony, I felt a tightness in my chest and my left arm grew rigid and pained, as if a line of needles were marching up it and closer to my heart. The numbness grew and the headache settled behind my eyes like iron weights. Deep in the recesses of my mind, I could hear something inchoate, perhaps attempting to take form, but whether it was the coming of music or not, I could not say.

I tried to continue my duties as usual, and Asterion was so distracted he didn't notice. I kept a smile on my face.

Four days before the youths would meet Asterion, the pain slipped from my body like water from a tipped pitcher. But there was something new, something of which I could make no sense. I began, involuntarily, to mimic Asterion. First, just in small movements, a twitch of the lip, a shuffle of the foot, a sigh or cough. Asterion still did not notice anything awry. At first I could distract him after copying some inconsequential motion by doing something immediately after, such as moving a piece of furniture or asking him about the weather.

Whatever had been in my mind had disappeared, leaving no trace.

Three days before the sacrifice, I began shadowing him completely. This he could not help but notice. I had no control over my body. I lost the power of speech and could not explain to him that I was possessed by some inexplicable and unseen force. I could not even express with my face my consternation and confusion. Whatever Asterion's face did, mine did. Identical clouds of astonishment, irritation, and then vexation crossed our visages. I could not fight it physically, and my spirit shortly thereafter followed. Though I was relieved to be rid of the torment of the previous days, this joining with Asterion was uncanny, disquieting beyond compare.

Then two days before the cleansing, my body no longer shadowed Asterion, but, how can I say it, *it foreshadowed* him. Whatever he was *about* to do, I did first. If he was going to lie down on the cool floor, I did it first. If he was going to stretch and yawn, I stretched and yawned first. Though our house, it is true, did not follow all the laws of logic, this was of a completely different flavor than Asterion appearing in different rooms of the labyrinth. All those Asterions were also the real, one Asterion. Yet each moved and thought with an individual will, as if the one Asterion was as dense as a hundred people, but without being heavier, without being burdened. They all fit somehow within, simultaneously, in Asterion.

Yes, Asterion had always referred to me affectionately as *the other Asterion,* but this was taking it too far.

One day passed with me performing every action of Asterion's in advance. What could I do but surrender? Inside, I began to weep for the loss of my freedom, however limited it might have seemed. What began to take the place of my will was a seed of an unexpected feeling. While I had always had affection and regard for my ward, I would not have said what I felt toward him was what was growing within me. Surely, I thought, this was love. His whole being became something like music to me. Never farther from him than an arm's length, but never closer, I began to sense that I was fulfilling some new purpose. Once he accepted the new reality, Asterion himself seemed happier than ever. He seemed translucent, and once, when he turned in the late afternoon light, I thought that I could even see through him to the space beyond, for just a moment. A space that seemed to lose all its edges. Perhaps I was becoming Asterion's soul.

A faint suggestion of the music of my childhood returned to me, at the periphery of my consciousness and memory.

On the morning of the day, I / he walked to the edge of the prison and as I / he put my / his face in the air, I / he sensed a shift in the wind. There was a new odor, faint but distinct, of salt on the wind. And something else very subtle, complex, something that I / he could not identify. An animal? Some kind of rare flower? I / he experienced a strange charge throughout my / his body, as if the air around the labyrinth became ever so slightly heavier. As if the earth below us became denser, tugging, holding us tight.

Never let me go, I said to myself.

Never let me go, Asterion said to himself.

*

*   *

Part Four: Unfurl Before Us
The morning came, as did the nine youths.

The music, or truly the desire for music, grew stronger within me, like a kind of pressure, pushing outward. My skin felt tight.

For the first time, I did not greet the youths and guide them to the center, because it was not something Asterion would have done. We were waiting in the middle of the labyrinth. Our breathing was steady. Our bodies felt light as air. We had thoughts of Ariadne and our childhood, hiding in the servants' rooms and running through the long halls, up and down the stairs. In our mind's eye, we saw rich fields of golden wheat and seas of green grass. It seemed to be the height of summer, when you could almost hear all the living things growing and ripening in the good warmth of the sun. In the azure sea, each wavelet rose like the back of a horse at an easy gallop and subsided in perfect sympathy with its brothers.

After a time, footsteps approached.

I heard the whistling of a tune that became bolder as it came closer—it was music, it echoed and came closer.

The boys entered the chamber. The passageway behind them remained in shadow. Our eyes took them in and Asterion was the first to notice something queer.

One youth, who was whistling the song, taller and more heavily built than the others, strode forward. We saw his handsome, human face. His dark eyes steady.

How unusual, thought I, wrinkling my brow. *How unusual,* thought Asterion, wrinkling his brow.

Ariadne would laugh, we thought, *because she loves surprises.*

We've dreamt of that tune, we thought, *feeling something inside us catch ablaze.*

The beautiful youth advanced. A roaring white noise entered our bull-ears.

The thought, *my name means star,* came to us.

Time rippled toward us, bearing down.

We saw our old tapestry unfurl before us.

The whistling stopped, and there was a brief after-sound.

The last thing we saw before the world disappeared was the blinding dazzle of a blade and a small ball of fine thread, its delicate tail leading away from us.

Exactly Like You

The words he uttered were no longer understandable, apparently,
although they seemed clear enough to him.
—Franz Kafka, *Die Verwandlung / The Metamorphosis*

You've had yourself stolen, haven't you?
There is someone who looks exactly like you, isn't there?
—Kim So-un, "The Disowned Student,"
The Story Bag: A Collection of Korean Folktales

It is now known that a fetus dreams.

Infants make memories, memories not accessible to the older mind, but perhaps to other systems of the body, older systems than our frontal lobe and other parts of our brain that developed later in our evolution.

Dreams occur during REM sleep, which, according to Dr. Charles P. Pollak, director of the Center for Sleep Medicine at New York-Presbyterian/Weill Cornell hospital, is "an evolutionarily old type of sleep that occurs at all life stages, including infancy, and even before infancy, in fetal life."[3]

We cannot find our original ~~family~~ is unknown to us. No access to stories about our fetal life, or to the body of the mother who was the creator, protector, and nurturer of that our life. We were with ~~her~~ Her until we were about _____ . We were breast-fed and bonded.

---

3. Charles P. Pollak, "Q&A Baby Dreams," an interview by C. Claiborne Ray, *New York Times* website, published November 22, 2005, http://query.nytimes.com/gst /fullpage.html?res=9C0CE0D81F3EF931A15752C1A9639C8B63.

Did you know that fetuses have a developed sense of smell? And, as soon as three days after birth, newborns are able to recognize their own mother's amniotic fluid. The indelibility of the scent of maternal milk follows soon after—at two weeks old, a baby can distinguish her mother's breast milk from that of another. Though we humans often give less attention to our sense of smell than we do to other senses (sight, sound, touch), for babies—and perhaps all of us at all stages of our lives—it is primary. For at least the first two months of life, a baby prefers the unmistakable scent of her own mother to any other odor.

We were born in or around May of 19__. Unknown are our ~~birth date~~ or our ~~name~~. Slipperiness of a ~~shared~~ time. One is an object, easily laundered and transferred. Relocated and reassigned. Physically safe, perhaps, and fed and sheltered, but without one's first materials and self and home: one's mother, one's *ur-body*.

A few months after our birth, on August 15, 1974, Park Chung-hee, the military dictator of South Korea, who had declared himself "president for life," was the target of an assassination attempt by Mun Se-gwang. This violent incident resulted in the death-by-gunfire of Park's wife, Yuk Young-soo, and a high school student who was part of a choir performing at the ceremony.

Our country, a people with a continuous history of over five thousand years, has been left divided since the end of the Korean War, that peninsula-wide trauma that resulted in tens of thousands of children being made available for adoption to the West, first to the U.S. The profound disruption of the end of Japan's colonial occupation, the brutal civil war, and the aftermath orchestrated by the U.S. resulted in unprecedented political and social change.

Perhaps our father and mother were people from the north, refugees to the south, ultimately trapped below the thirty-eighth parallel. Perhaps they were married but we were the fourth child, one too many. Perhaps our mother was raped by a taxi driver. Perhaps our parents were involved in an extramarital affair and could not be together. Perhaps our father died, or moved away.

Park's daughter, Park Geun-hye, now sixty years old, who was a young woman of twenty-two when we were born, was very recently elected president of the Republic of Korea, the first woman to hold this office. She, being the daughter of a dictator, among other things, is a figure of controversy. Underneath (or merely behind) the machinery of politics, we wonder what dreams her mother, Young-soo, had while she was pregnant with Geun-hye. What maternal stamps and stains marked her, competed or melded with Chung-hee's heritable contributions? Could they have predicted that the mother, the First Lady of a despot, would give way, in this manner, to the daughter?

*

Traditional beliefs regarding fetal life:

> Koreans count the gestation period as the first year in a child's life.

> It is believed that the mother's thoughts, behaviors, and feelings during the pregnancy will have a formative influence on the well-being of the fetus, so the prenatal period is called the education period for the unborn child.

> A dream may predict the kind of person the unborn child will be.

> Someone very close to the child to be born—the mother, grandfather, or other close relative—is likely to have such a significant premonition-like dream.[4]

During the second six or seven months of our life outside the womb, in our *post*-fetal life, we surely dreamed. We also experienced three families, three mothers during that time. A foster family cared for us until we were adopted by an American couple, to which we were delivered at the age of thirteen months, or, about one year in American-time, while, in Korean-time, we were over two years old.

Now we ourselves are a mother, with a daughter and a son. We remember well their slow fetal metamorphoses. Our sleep was highly interrupted by various expected discomforts.
Did we loan them our sleep? What dreams did we give them?

Many fetal dreams never make it outside the womb. The making of a human—our large brains, those frontal lobes, that capacity for memory, planning, and cruelty—is energy-intensive and complicated. Many things can go awry.

Apparently, many embryos "know" there is something wrong with them and thus efficiently self-destruct, making way for the next embryo that may have a better chance at survival outside the womb's plush red palace.

*

4. Hyun Sook Han, *Understanding My Child's Korean Origins* (Minneapolis Children's Home Society of Minnesota, 1983).

In Greek mythology, the god of dreams, Morpheus, was winged and could assume any form. His domain, δῆμος ὀνείρων, the land of dreams, was near the underworld, home to Night and her children. Dreams departed Morpheus's realm through two gates.

Poets often referred to the two gates leading from this dominion of dreams. The gates were made from the protection, the ferocity, of animals. One gate—ivory (ἐλέφας / *elephas*), one gate—horn (κέρας / *keras*). The dreams themselves were divided; truth through the horn half-door, false dreams passed by the ivory gate. The natural world enclosed, protected, and opened out to give the dreams freedom. Ever inside the gated domain stood an elm tree that served as a kind of coatrack for the winged dreams made by the Oneiroi. These dreams hung there with their secrets.

As we task our memory-organ to re-member our life in Korea, we breed dream after dream. False dreams? Truthful dreams? Hanging? Phantom shaped? They drop like ripe fruit, then disappear before hitting the ground, preventing bruising, rotting. Dreams are ephemera and have no body to violate, no flesh to decay. They can remain fresh as the wind, recycled like hot rising vapor from the ocean, into the frozen clouds, and eventually back into the crashing black water, the source of all dreams, the living body of our planet.

*

A few years ago, we had our first dream set in Korea in which everyone, including us, was speaking Korean. A grandmother and a hut and a doorway figured prominently. There might have been a fire. There might have been daylight. It was brief but vivid.

We woke up changed, an altered person. Transformed.

In Kafka's *The Metamorphosis,* Gregor Samsa awakens one morning to find that he has become a monstrous vermin (*Ungeziefer*: an unclean beast not fit for sacrifice). Readers are not privy to the transformation itself, nor to any rational explanation for the radical change. It can be read as, among many other things, a metaphor for the arbitrariness of punishment in an indifferent, hostile universe. Though there is a hospital right across the street from his room, no attempt is made to either bring Gregor there or fetch a doctor from it. It looms, inaccessible.

Another meaning of the transformation, which is not mutually exclusive with other readings, is that Gregor has become, in body, that which he was "in soul," something akin to a beetle, a mindless drudge carrying food from world to nest, over and over again. Gregor, a traveling salesman, brings money home to his family, again and again. The Samsa family lives in a society that is primarily an impersonal bourgeois economy, a culture that values commerce over every other human activity.

Late in the story, a large, bony, wild haired "char woman" (a stand-in for the archetypal witch, although bemused and practical rather than wicked and rapacious) addresses Gregor as "you old dung beetle." Dung beetles live on the dung from other animals and can roll dung balls many times their own weight. Some dung beetles also eat decayed vegetation, similar to Gregor, who found that he preferred rotting food to the food he used to enjoy in his previous form. A metamorphosis (the Greek words for "change" and "form") is one of the dung beetle's life stages. A dung beetle may begin its life as an egg inside a dung ball. The egg hatches and the larva eats the dung for its nourishment until it emerges from the ball a fully formed adult—a singular evolution.

By the time *The Metamorphosis* was published in 1915, Darwin's *The Origin of Species* had been in circulation for fifty-six years.

In Kafka's tale, Gregor devolves. He is transformed during sleep, and he spends the rest of his brief life in his bedroom, a space in which one should experience nightly rejuvenation but instead offers Gregor only a terminal prison cell. It becomes a den that accretes dust and filth, its furniture irrelevant as Gregor enjoys crawling on the walls and ceilings as he can no longer lie comfortably in bed, cannot sit on his settee or at his desk. By the end of his wretched, solitary life spent working to pay off his parents' debt (the German word *Schuld* means both "debt" and "guilt"), he has shrunken, and his body can be placed into a small box. A paper coffin, like a grave made of something as flimsy as words. Easily hidden, buried, burned.

Gregor was abandoned—by his employer, father, mother, sister, and ultimately one could argue, his god. Did he transcend? Did he ask for it? Did he have it coming, with his ridiculous delusions of self-importance and his complaints and his small-mindedness and his obsession with his sister's changing states of un/dress? Did he transcend by the end of his life—with his radiant embrace of music, with his peaceful, solitary death in the light?

Abandoned and then re-en-familied, re-kinned, an adoptee is many things, including, I would posit, both a form of ongoing transit and a re-territory, a re-form. This form takes on different meanings depending on the place, the language, and the people looking, listening. If our form is different, if we are no longer recognizable, if no one speaks our language, who are we?

*

How important is memory?

The online *Stanford Encyclopedia of Philosophy* has this to say about memory, an explanation of its complexity that comforts us and somewhat affirms our preoccupation with our fetal psychic amnesia: "Remembering is often suffused with emotion, and is closely involved in both extended affective states such as love and grief, and socially significant practices such as promising and commemorating. It is essential for much reasoning and decision making, both individual and collective. It is connected in obscure ways with dreaming. Some memories are shaped by language, others by imagery. Much of our moral and social life depends on the peculiar ways in which we are embedded in time. Memory goes wrong in mundane and minor, or in dramatic and disastrous ways."

Our fetal dreams, our memories, while unworded by us—and mundane, minor in the scheme of things—coalesce to form something: the abandoned, a student of ourself, a stranger, a double, one disowned and re-owned, winged, made of polished horn, in debt, haunted by guilt, monstrous, arbitrary, punished, rewarded, nameless, and renamed.

Harness

Facts   Flesh ghost

입앙 인니다.

[*bowing*]

만마서 반갑습니다. *Mannaseo bangapseumnida*

It's nice to meet you.

How should I address you?

To Say

"The Korean language strictly reflects the hierarchical order. Speech styles are divided according to a system of honorifics, and this system is complex and richly textured. In fact, it may well be that no language on earth has a more finely differentiated system of honorifics."[5]

Drown

The bi-archy. Doppelgänger. The woman who split away. Mutually unintelligible. An order of intimate estrangement.

Meet. When bending over a simple plate of water. Through the gates.

---

5. Iksop Lee and S. Robert Ramsey, *The Korean Language* (New York: State University of New York Press, 2000), 224.

The gorgeous, drowned *oneironautics*.

If we speak in tongues. Sewn to my heel.

What

All these wild breakers to recede.

Water

Graveyard of names. Deck of cards. Stone teeth.

Leaks and bursts, a balloon, a boat, a floating thing.

Blanks

Occupation era. Hermit no more.

Invasions

Mongols (1231)

Japanese (1592)

Manchus (1627)

Japan

Three stages of the Japanese Colonial Era:[6]

1. "the dark age of" <u>Subjugation</u> (1910–19) "where the military ruled by threat and violence"

2. <u>Cultural accommodation</u> (1920–31) "after the Korean Independence Movement in March 1919" "allowing some freedom in schools, newspapers, and businesses"

---

6. Hildi Kang, *Under the Black Umbrella: Voices from Colonial Korea, 1910–1945* (Ithaca, New York: Cornell University Press, 2005).

3. <u>Assimilation</u> (1931–45) "renewed tightening of controls and forced participation in the Japanese war effort"

Ur-Father

Born thirteen years after 박정희 Park Chung-hee seized power in a coup d'état and two years after he instituted military rule declaring himself president for life. Three months and two days after our birthday: assassination. Uncompleted. He was missed but not his wife. *Stray bullet, enter me and destroy me.* Later that day, she died.

Documented

9 p.m. on January 20, 1975, at the Holt Office in Seoul, Korea. Processed at the Shin-Kyo Police Station.

신 (Shin)

Knocked loose.

Family of one.

At seven months old, I become the chief and sole member of (my new branch of) the Shin family.

"Shin is a Korean family name. It is cognate to the Chinese family names Shen and Xin. According to the 2000 census in South Korea, there were 911,556 people carrying the Shin surname."[7]

---

7. World Public Library, "Shin (Korean Name)," accessed February 20, 2016, http://www.worldlibrary.org/articles/shin_(korean_name).

"No Record"

Orphan 호적 (hojuk). In her article "Our Adoptee, Our Alien: Transnational Adoptees as Specters of Family and Foreignness in Korea," Eleana Kim explains how the "orphan hojuk" and the legal "orphanization" process reconstitutes the adoptee socially in Korea. Within "the context of Korean law, she becomes a person with the barest of social identities, and in the context of Korean cultural norms, she lacks the basic requirements of social personhood—namely, family lineage and genealogical history."

The "orphan hojuk," or the family registry created so that we could be separated legally from our Korean family and made available for intercountry adoption. The first is an English translation of the second. What we have is a hasty and terrible photocopy, dark and illegible, the Korean original. Yet, an original of what?

Deformation, a defamation in a home country. *An ill report, rumor, scandal.* A secret.
We are a copy and an original.
We will make a record.

HO JUK DEUNG BON (FAMILY REGISTRATION)

Date: **Feb. 25, 1975**

Permanent Address: # 382-14 Hap Jung Dong, Ma Po Ku, Seoul, Korea
Previous Family Chief : No Record

The following family is established as of this date **Feb. 17, 1975**
in accordance with the investigation conducted by the Chief Officer of Ma Po District Office and
therefore duly registered.

Family Chief: **Shin, Sun Yung**

Relation to Previous Family Chief : No Record

Father   :   No Record

Mother   :   No Record

Sex   :   **Female**

Date of Birth: **May 12, 1974**

Family Origin:

This family **Shin** and family origin **Pyung San** are given in accordance
with the permission by the Court of Home Affairs of Seoul as of this date **Feb. 10, 1975**.

This is to certify that the above statement is full, true and correct copy of
The Original Family Register.

Signed by **Yong Hee Park**
Chief Officer
Ma Po District Office
Seoul, Korea

This is a full, true and correct translation of the attached certified copy of
HO JUK DEUNG BON (FAMILY REGISTRATION).

Choi, Young Hee

Holt Children's Services
Seoul, Korea

Korean
Hojuk
(Family Registry)

In these copies, light escapes at the corners.

Sudden

We are a colony of one.

Though the καταστροφών, *katastrofón,* catastrophes of war were over, mothers were still compelled to ~~leave their children in the forest eat~~ send their children far across the sea.

καταστροφή. *An overturning. To turn down. To trample on.*

A sudden end.

Ride

Dark forest and beyond / steal fire from skulls. Mother dead, her gift of a magic talking doll deep in our trembling pocket. Cotton wool silent mouth. Beautiful Vassalisa. Our broom, enigma, to sweep thought from every corner.

> All day she walked on. Towards evening she came to a glade. She looked into the glade and saw a hut; all round it was a fence made from human bones.
>
> On the fence were human skulls; human legbones served instead of a gate, there were hands instead of bolts, and sharp teeth acted as the lock. At this sight the girl was terrified: she stood rooted to the ground.
>
> Suddenly a horseman rode past; he was dressed entirely in black, was riding a black horse, and the horse's harness, too, was black. He galloped up to

the gate and vanished as if he had been swallowed into the earth. Night came on.[8]

To beg > borrow > burn.

A coup d'état of this, abandonment, miniature καταστροφή!

Immigration as it comes on and on like black Night on its black horse. These pages our glade and our harness.

---

8. *Russian Folk Tales,* trans. H. C. Stevens (London: Hamlyn, 1967).

Orphan: The Plural Form

The women laughed and wept; the crowd stamped their feet
enthusiastically, for at that moment Quasimodo was really beautiful.
He was handsome—this orphan, this foundling, this outcast.
—Victor Hugo, *The Hunchback of Notre-Dame*

Orphan. Conjuring, for some, images of dirty, ill-clothed children from the nineteenth century. Dickens. It is an old-fashioned word. Technically most Korean adoptees are not orphans—in most cases we did not become "available for adoption" due to parental death.

In Microsoft Word, "adoptees" is underlined in little red Vs that look like the stitching that ran across some of our dresses when we were younger. Red, forbidden, dangerous, bloody.

Word does not recognize the plural form of *adoptee.*

If you control-click on *adoptees,* the first word in the drop-down list is Help. Then comes *adoptee, adopters, adopted, adopter.* For some reason, Add is grayed out in our list and we cannot add *adoptees* to our dictionary. We can, however, Ignore All. Or AutoCorrect or click on Spelling . . . both of which bring us to the aforementioned list. When we typed *refugees, amputees, tutees* . . . they all remained unlined.

*

*   *

A poor mother who was from a poor country.

"Third World."

We were told that the poverty was so severe when we were born that the government made it legal to abandon one's child to an institution such as a hospital, police station, or social agency.

The story of our country's struggles and our mothers' misfortunes began and ended there for some of us: dusty rings around the planet-word *orphan*.

Orphan is a gorgeous word. Sublime. The first syllable *or* reminds me of gold ore, or simply the word *or*, which means the possibility of alternatives, the certainty that another choice is to follow the little word *or*. English has so many of these tiny words that mean so much—*and, the, an, if, so* . . .

The word *orphan* probably comes from the Latin *orbus*, which means *bereaved*. We love how when you want to indicate the word itself you italicize it. The word gets dressed up, leans into the wind, gets seemingly darker, moves forward, speeds itself to mean The Word and not the word.

When you type in the word *adoptee* into the Online Etymology Dictionary search, you get this: "No matching terms found." But of course it's from *adoption*, L. *adoptare*, "to choose for oneself." *Adoptee* then implies that one has been chosen for someone else's self.

Adoptee is a word that sounds unfinished.

The long double *ee* sound resonates against the hard palate inside the pink, ridged cave of the mouth, the tongue lying down, the tip touching the back of the bottom front teeth, the jaws slightly open, the lips apart. The skull vibrates for just a moment after the sound itself is gone.

It is a word that refers to a permanent exchange; it refers to the choice of the adopter; it defines the adoptee as an artifact, something created by will. Or force. Or chance. Or inevitability.

*

*   *

The Big Bang. Matter exploding and each particle drifting away from one another. A family as triangle. Drifting lines. This [mother-father-child] triangle will never be reassembled. All of these ghostly relationships.

"How can I heal if I can't feel time?" ponders Leonard Shelby in the Christopher Nolan neo-noir film *Memento*. Shelby has anterograde amnesia, which means he is unable to make new memories and retain them. He remembers everything up to the concussion and traumatic event, or so he claims.

We are all time travelers. We travel at the speed of one hour every hour, one year every year. The light we see from the sun is eight minutes old. We are bathed in, we live from, energy coming to us from the past.

We need more than eight minutes to get back to our body before it was a body, when it was our origin. We think that if we keep trying to get closer and closer to those non-memories that we will go back in time and change the course of events.

But there's nothing but blankness.

A kind of blackness that fades outward but has a sound. It has the sound of a wall, a thick wall, and we can hear muffled voices on the other side. They are so close, if only they knew we were here, in this room.

The foreigner is a "symptom" (Danièle Lochak): psychologically he signifies the difficulty we have of living as an *other* and with others; politically, he underscores the limits of nation-states and of the national political conscience that characterizes them and that we have all deeply interiorized to the point of considering it normal that there are foreigners, that is, people who do not have the same rights as we do.

—Julia Kristeva, "By What Right Are You a Foreigner?"
Strangers to Ourselves

I have been a stranger here in my own land: All my life.
—Antigone, *Antigone* by Sophocles

The Error of Blood Relation

—based on "Antigone's Nature" by William Robert

Where is this criminal?

Brother, cadaver
across her mortal limits
    and the terrain of the impossible
we can follow her strange latitudes

Why doesn't she fly?

Antigone, sister-daughter
the uncradled, the unbride
    bear her name
tame her, dazzling this line of sight

Were we born to love?

flight through the palace, an arrow through Ismene
oil on the body, dust on the body
    birds and dogs unmasking
a cadaver named brother

What is a king for?

traitor the body the loudness of duty
Polynices, did you think the throne would fit down your throat alone?
    brave river of men behind you
a wonderland of death

Is it better to know?

woman-child, relieve us of our weather full of battle luster
a child of incest resists traditional lines of genealogy
the sky was a bright choir of gold
a carnival of brothers

We love war?

soldiers losing their names
gods, leave us to make my name fray
my brother, fury
form and torn

Can't you be quiet and just live?

Antigone, speaking and acting from the other side
beyond altars and thrones, into the crypt of heart and home
a woman who improperly speaks
who makes marriage with the systematically fatal

Take me with you.

wakes the brother from the cadaver, disappearing boat
what blood and threat heaves us across the threshold, household
we walk every barrens for fidelity to the dead
feeding fine on our common loss, any cost

Don't leave me here alone.

      incest and the last dress hanging
in your virgin's closet
      hoarding conjugal surplus and in debt to its final price
where have we courted this sexed dialectic

I don't know if I'm a woman here, at last.

      subjects severing suffering
are we ruined citizens
      any contested king of balm and sin
the error of blood relation

The mother of my own death.

      Antigone, a new mother, asunder
some heavy ledger
      to taint and tear you, make you cave and kin
my sister of unbearable splendor

Until death do us unite . . .

      daughter of cadavers
your wedding underground
      a dire foreign bargain
make yourself a stranger, now with your betrothed

Father, mother, brothers, I've brought you my eyes . . .

      now with your brother
all together dining on the dark

I Will Make an Example

—based on "Antigone Claimed: 'I Am a Stranger!' Political Theory and the Figure of the Stranger" by Andrés Fabián Henao Castro

a lush surrender

fortified excess

expense the spectator, wash in gold

settler, rape this treaty

womanize punishment

burn the dispossessed and their illegal sentiments

useful outcast

visionary museum of artifice

willful Antigone riding a floating cemetery

daughter and brother and father and war

the last alibi

inside me breeds a bounty of sentinels

column and sanction

a civilian's dream

strange new tomb, O dear god, I have no home

beg in my territory

the ground a vast altar, a table

all the dead bodies kept alive, permanent occupation

binge on sovereignty

contagion, quarantine, forty days and forty nights

natal (arsenal) to her marital (immortal)

homo logos

agon; the need for the word *native*

sideshow body of the exile, dirge and discipline

The Limit Case

—based on "Bringing Antigone Home?" by Valerie Reed

Is Antigone the original cyborg?

The limits of woman, human. Everything put to the test.

She was born into a kind enclosure, like an animal born in captivity, her own family folded in on itself. The dollhouse with no windows. When having a king for a father is a death sentence. Essence before existence? She is eternal and so I will speak of her in the present tense.

Antigone is like a compass that points underground, always drawing her closer and closer to her home. The tide, inexorable. The cave into which she is banished opens up for her like a wound and heals around her. Or perhaps it is like a flower turning toward the sun. Haemon, like a bee, goes in for the nectar and gets enclosed in the petals as they close for the night. Haemon, good son, tries to save his father.

But Creon, through free will, becomes his own one-man plague. He gives birth to death. Antigone, mother of herself, cyborg, executes her self-destruct program. Gets up, wears a different woman's body in every space and time, and does it all over again. In Korean, in French, in English. Every time I see her I eat all her technology and spit the death out; it is hers alone, she fought for it, and she made it herself with her own veil. What is the last thing each of us will wear on our last day?

Haemon, always the bridesmaid, never the bride, consummates his marriage with his own sword, plunges it into his own body, with father as witness, father as almost-victim. Why does he kill himself? Is he just a pawn in the gods' punishment of Creon? An object to be taken away to force Creon into an empty room in which to live out the rest of his miserable life?

The oedipal blindness was contagious. Creon and Tiresias and his boy made a triangle, but Creon wouldn't take the eye in time. He threw it across the floor, but it was too late. In everyone's heart he thought he saw money hunger, betrayal, disobedience.

As a woman, Antigone was born disobedient. How dare anyone not be born a man? But sons don't grow on trees. Sometimes hillsides, with their ankles pierced, bawling, abandoned. Outside, strangers. The sky my protean ceiling everywhere I go. Antigone and her survivor sister, Ismene, dare to be seen by us, the audience of Athenian citizens (men) outside the palace. They slip into the building and head straight for the altar, the space of sacrifice.

Altar, θυσιαστήριον, thusiastérion. The meeting place between god and worshiper. In Latin, *adolēre + altus*. Get high, Antigone, then get low. The meeting place is Polynices's body. Let the river take you to your family. Leave Ismene above to remind Creon of those he banished and those who abandoned him, he, a man of excess almost equal to Antigone's excess.

What is a cyborg but a hybrid creature of excess? A thing that exceeds the sum of its parts. A thing that has extended its powers, enhanced, even superpowered. Antigone, the supernatural. The uncanny. *Unheimlich,* Freud's word. Un-home-like. Antigone the homeless, Antigone the stranger, Antigone the royal, Antigone, *in place of mother.*

A woman is like a hollow horse. All made of doors. All made of space.

The Sphinx was a cyborg, a hybrid monster. She was obsessed with men, made his life a riddle.

Antigone, the envoy of ghosts. Antigone the enhanced, her life everywhere at once, outside and inside the palace, with her brother's body aboveground, her parents and other brother below. Like a god she is ubiquitous.

Many of us know something about transgression. Something is wrong about us. What can we do but embrace the makeshift, assemble ourselves as we go, sometimes the punishment exceeding the crime.

Antigone doesn't actually exist. She is not the hero of the play named after her. She is in flight, she drags a machinery of re-territorialization with her like a kind of harrow, digging a long narrow grave behind her. She is invisible, transparent, already dead the minute she walks onto the stage.

During the one and only performance of *Antigone* during Sophocles's time, she was not even a woman. Men in their wigs and masks and high heels. Pity and fear. Catharsis. Women play women now. Antigone is more woman than woman, more man than man. She is a machine pretending to be a disobedient girl.

When I think of myself as mostly machine, my disobedience becomes completely natural. Tiresias was at one time a woman, and now he sees everything. He remembers the future.

In the play, we never meet Antigone in the underworld. We are only with her until she is sealed up in the cave (bridal chamber, labor-and-delivery room, funeral parlor, tomb).

She is excessive. She is eternal. Hybrid of life and death.

A disobedient woman. A machine at home.

Predictably, Asia functions in *Blade Runner* as the alluring
and foreign "other" of the West, the normal, and the present:
it is the extra kick that makes the near future look like "New York
on a bad day" to quote the director—dirty, overcrowded, full of
freaks, the poor, and people of color. Yet not so predictably, this
"other" also is linked with the morally ambiguous hero
(and yes, Deckard is a replicant).

—Jane Chi Hyun Park,
on her book *Yellow Future: Oriental Style in Hollywood Cinema*
in a November 20, 2011, interview in *Rorotoko*

I want to see [the Voight-Kampff empathy test]
work on a person. I want to see it work on a negative before
I provide you with the positive.

—Dr. Eldon Tyrell, *Blade Runner*

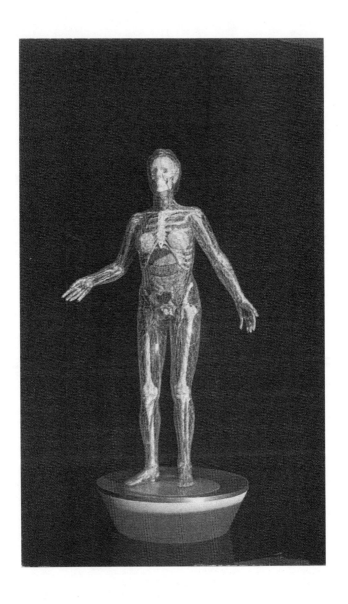

In the Other Future

1. As a child there were many field trips to the Robert Crown Center for Health Education in Hinsdale, Illinois. I remember nothing except Valeda, the TAM (Transparent Anatomical Manikin); she lived there on a platform on a stage in a dark room. She was made by a German medical artist. There were others of her around the country and in Europe. I only ever met her, not the others.

2. She was a teacher. She lit up. She told me not to be afraid to be manufactured. To be immortal until I wasn't. Like me, she could talk without moving her mouth.

3. To be assembled and disassembled.

4. To dis-ease and dis-order.

5. To be a modern child. To be worth your weight in gold.

6. To be worth less and less as you grow older, to be an old, cheap child.

7. Abject, object, select.

8. There once were two anatomical manikins, twins. The one on the left did all the talking, the one on the right had no face. The one on the left was muscles and organs. The one on the right was bones.

9. Everyone can see through me. Everyone can see all the people inside me. In my computer model, which can separate into

layers, there are so many different people inside me, I myself haven't even met them all yet. My twin to the left of me, or the right of me. One of me has a face, one of me can talk to the audience.

10. Can the whole world see me all at once?

11. I'm living in the future. I have also left myself behind. As if there's a front and a back, as if time were like walking through the back door of a house and out through the front. As if there were rooms and floors inside. As if time were a flood filling all the rooms and closets, breaking the windows and making everything touch everything else all at once.

12. The positive me is testing the negative me, always asking me questions and trying to trick me into believing it is human, or that I am human, or that we are both machines. All of these machines inside us: lungs, heart, gut, brain, eyes, everything moving of their own volition. A flock of birds, a pack of wolves. I am like one hundred electric eels. Our skin is an extravagant tongue, tasting everything, making the dark things inside us jealous. Those stealthy sea creatures, always plotting and scheming, rarely giving me the news.

13. In the future, no one is completely human. Some people never tire of upgrading. I wanted wings until all the countries moved into the air.

14. I let Deckard rape me so, you know, it wasn't rape. *I remember playing the piano at home. I remember having my picture taken.* Being a replicant means you never have to be a powerless child. You never have to be old. Time moves around you, but you never

change. You have less than the life span of a pet dog but look how well people treat their dogs.

15. If I were a dog I would mate with a wolf. Devolve. I think humans remember being wild, too. I could eat all this light and turn into a white room.

16. I didn't know I wasn't human. My past was invented, implanted, and accepted. I'm more real than you are because I know I'm not real.

17. Empty orchestra. You can see through me, you can trust me, I have nothing to hide, I'm right here, I'm not going anywhere.

Like a Second Person inside Us

Gorgon, guardian, weapon—our armor like a second person out-
    side us

*   *
        *

Now eyes, in the end, breakable
A bouldering heart, a cave like a sister inside her
Eat the whip, the privilege

*   *
        *

Our bones like a second person inside us
Caves and brides, this unblooded
Bed, Antigone and her irreplaceable _____

*   *
        *

Unburied, the broken king
A father with scars
At the ankles like buttons

Abiding his skin, his prophecy like an unborn child inside us
A gallery, atlas
Judge of the dead, we are on the stage, we are at the altar . . .

*   *
        *

Shade mother bound in beeswax to mechanical father
The sport of sword falling
Ocean's trenches swallow to ravish

Sheet of sun gold
Hammered above, behind you, lonely oracle
The Minotaur's roaring heart

*   *
          *

Between dynasty and doors in the universe
Porches of the spirit
The nest we pluck from the hedge like a dried flower

Fireflies candling, the jar
A glass bead, an eye a liquid room swimming inside us
An urn of watery light to drink and drink

*   *
          *

Our bones like a cabinet locked narrow inside us
Organs of the secret life
Campfire ash or rebellion of moths

Powder and pollen, my baby turning to chalk
A starry crown of bees, bits of hive
And honey in the wind

*   *
          *

The body a sweet factory, a pyre
Our bones will harbor a fire like a second person inside us
An unfixed form, a phoenix for hire

A tempest brings all
Orphans home, follow
The dark veins and plumes of planetary skin

*   *
    *

The weighted grains of the flightless
Our bones felted and feathered like a second person inside us
A hundred thousand eyes

Glass the horizon like a captain
These paper woods all a tumble
Each trunk a curved boat of time

*   *
    *

Your mind no more than a mushroom
A burrow, branch, floating motes make a wedding dress, white
    inside us
From stars callous

To receive now, a gorgeous garment
A robe and a family
To wear it on our backs, mantle of atoms

*   *
    *

Our bones evolving: step-by-step a more specialized person inside us
Our very own Darwin, beaks and seeds
It won't be long now

This combustion dwindles, hurries to adapt
Before the next glacial age, ice birthing and calving, a frozen ocean
    inside us
Before the long night of dreams in reverse, inside out, in the invis-
    ible orchestra

Autoclonography

for performance

> In 1998, scientists in South Korea claimed to have successfully
> cloned a human embryo, but said the experiment was interrupted very
> early when the clone was just a group of four cells. In 2002, Clonaid,
> part of a religious group that believes humans were created by extra-
> terrestrials, held a news conference to announce the birth of what it
> claimed to be the first cloned human, a girl named Eve. However, de-
> spite repeated requests by the research community and the news media,
> Clonaid never provided any evidence to confirm the existence of this
> clone or the other twelve human clones it purportedly created.
> —National Human Genome Research Institute, "Cloning Fact Sheet"

1.

the sonographic fetus is a *cyborg*—clonograph—dear future clones
you are multiple—to use the letter *s* to *make more of someone*—to
use the letter *s* to make a *very small silent black river*—into which
many *babies have been borne away*—and into the river under the
river—the black ocean under the blue ocean—catacombs of bones
of those *delivered unto the shore* beneath the shore—as men of God
from Spain and *the Spain beneath Spain*—arrived with their ships
of *death beneath death*—the world under this world that *outnumbers
this world*

2.

dear future clones *I love you more*—than I love myself because there
are *more* of you—than there are of me although I am your mother—
and your sister and *your ancestor*—and look in the mirror at your
young face—and look behind you at my olding face—and you can
do something only prophets can do—which is to *see into the future*—

Τειρεσίας / Tiresias killed two snakes with a stick—*Hera punished him and changed his sex*—he was *turned into a woman*—he served Hera as a priestess, he got married to a man and had children—when he came upon two snakes again he decided to leave them alone—it *broke the curse*—he was turned back into a man

3.
to love the word *offspring*—*to spring from a trap to spring from jail*—*sperkhesthai* "to hurry" hurry spring come rain-shine—always spring in the wombs deployed for this purpose—ovaries are primed—the word *offspring* is really both singular and plural—the cell lines are cultured in the *singulary*—the word *single* will become a quaint idea *has become a quaint idea*—we won't need the letter *f* anymore in the middle of things—there will never be one knife or one self—*knives selves* doesn't that sound better *we are better together*—we won't need the word *I* anymore

to love the word *we* more than *I*—we don't have to capitalize *we* even in the middle of a sentence—the *I* has been *sprung from its prison* no more stretcher for you letter *I*—who do you think you are letter *I* to be so tall to be like the Roman numeral one—*you don't stand for one anymore*—you don't stand up anymore

you are small again a small *i* a short thing with a black dot for a face—we have always wanted a dot for a face—so much easier to look beautiful every day—if everyone's face is a dot then no one has to look beautiful every day—our dot is the same as your dot so why don't we exchange dots—no one will know the difference but *it might taste different behind the dot*—a little bit of different weather behind your dot yes—we have always wanted a manhole cover for a face—we have always wondered what is below the manhole—what keeps the city from flooding?—what keeps the ark half-built?—what keeps the animals from walking two by two by two by two?

4.

dear future clones we are *rethinking* about you—*electrically we are electrifying* you in the plural you—*neuronally we are neuronifying* you in the spaces between our neurons in the salt sea—inside our skulls *skol* said those death metal Vikings for skull—when they drank from the skulls of their defeated—mead from honey *mead from a queen* and so many, many baby bees everywhere—drunk on togetherness on doing being the same until they die—good bees they take out our bodies sweep them into the air, the air—that is heaven *that is a good death* dropping at the same rate together—duty done *skol skol skol*

we are picturing you in our mind as Athena born from her father's head—burst we like the word *burst*—and we want our head put back together—we want our head *not* split open like a watermelon—even if it meant we got to have *the daughter we always wanted*—even if we get the daughter without a mother—we don't need a mother we are father-mother—you only need one parent—and put the word *father* or the word *mother* on the shelves with the knives

5.

will we be taking *family photographs* together—we and you our future clones—how will we tell years later who is who is who is who is who is who—will we stand in the middle because we are the original—and you copies fan out around us in what kind of order— *who do we like the best today*—who does the photographer think has *the brightest twinkle* in their eye eye eye—do we all wear the same outfit where can we get so many of the same outfit—by then all the stores will sell so many of the same outfit—don't be ugly today or if you do don't go outside because we don't want anyone to see us— looking so ugly or shabby or old or female—*when you're looking so female older female just stay inside* nobody wants to see that—in such bright light at least bring some shade—or your shadow who isn't *the wrong color*—and your shadow no one can see our face our dot our aging dot not as dot-like as it used to be

6.

we have been making a documentary of these fetuses—sonograms just photographic slices now also 3-D imaging—*still all that blur* but no fetus is *the wrong color*—sometimes the wrong gender *the wrong gender in the dark*—sometimes the face the dot of the fetus is *facing away from us*—as if it doesn't want to see us doesn't want us to see *us ourselves their future our origins*

7.

in all the movies and television shows and books about clones—dear future clones they are always never actual clones—they are actors photographed again again again—but we are never fooled although *we love being fooled* all the time—we are afraid of the times we are not fooled—in our lives we don't actually own anything although *we pay* for things—we will pay for everything for you because you are our future—we didn't know we wanted to be *immortal*—but could you please not get yourselves into as much pain—we are worried about what all that pain will mean—*will it be our fault*—will it be our problem—will it be our future—my pain is your past but *you might forget me* I mean us we mean us

8.

to love the look of our own blood—*because it spelled things* it spells things for us—anything that was inside us recently *was* us—we know Freud would agree and Freud is *still inside* me meaning us— he might not want to be us—*he never dreamed about us*—Freud where are you in our body

you must be *in the blood* because it comes from *the basement inside our bones*—and we think you like basements the way you like talking and we feel you—clinging in your three-piece suit to the underside of an iceberg—*we will save you* from sea lions—there are things on the surface from *we cannot save*—we are loathe to *spill your blood* onto the blue-white milk ice floes—we are loathe to spill or spell

a flotilla of ships approaches—all alike all alike *one might save us*— one might take you with us Freud please come with us—all these years into your future *you never dreamed about us* even once—but we dream about you Freud we dream about *the world beneath the world*

9.

future clones, we did not know that Freud *took his own life*—where did he take it *he took it into the future*—but before he could take it into the future he had to break it off *from the animal*—now he is *the animal beneath the animal*—you offspring we never knew we could make so many animals essentially an infinite number—we could repopulate the earth with ourselves with *the right machines* includ-ing ourselves—we could reproduce ourselves and *train ourselves* to reproduce ourselves to reproduce ourselves—this could go on until someone stops us or our death drive *thank you Freud*—allows us to return to *the room beneath the room*—the body beneath our body that is exhausted—that is mere breath that is leaning heavily on the airlock—with its *cool metal wheel* against our hot olding face

10.

we apologize we are less like us in *all the ways we are like us* like you like us we are so so sorry—we just knew that we would let ourselves down but *we didn't know what else to do*—*we didn't want to take our lives* because we thought it would be better—to give them away to all of you—it's true that someone always has to pay

A particularly beautiful woman is a source of terror.
As a rule, a beautiful woman is a terrible disappointment.

—Carl Jung, in an interview with Frederick Sands,
Pittsburgh Post-Gazette, September 10, 1961

Because a baby's hands form early in gestation, researchers like to
say that they amount to a "fossilized record" of early development,
one that may provide insight into future well-being.

—Eleanor Smith, "Palm Reading Is Real? How Your Hands Actually
Predict Your Future," *The Atlantic,* July/August 2015

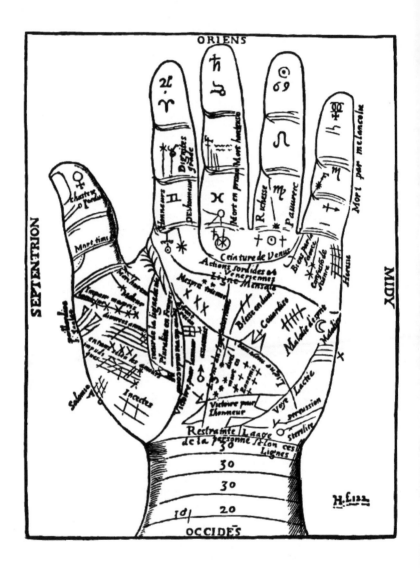

Unalloyed

Lambert: You admire it.

Ash: I admire its purity. A survivor . . . unclouded by conscience,
remorse, or delusions of morality.
—*Alien*

1. The woman in white by the side of the road will eat your blushing heart and throw your alien, illegible, edible laws into the fire.

2. The woman in white has a face like a weapon. Sharpen it. If you could get inside her body you could ride in it like a vast and war-ready ship. Slaves at the oars. Sections of time thrown overboard to lighten the load, for you will get heavier and heavier as time goes on.

3. The woman in white places her palms against your face, like twin curses, and leaves black marks all over your flesh, as if you were a herd animal being chosen for the next truck, which arrives tomorrow.

4. You invent the internal tattoo and gently remove each organ for scarification, branding, and the gentle and vivid watercolor of the sewing needle.

5. You would like to devour permanence and dissolve it in your many stomachs. You would like to replace your skin when you grow weary of its memories, everything that seeps in it and never passes through, never evaporates.

6. This woman is a disappointment. Can she be exchanged, can she be returned, can she be reborn. Douse it again.

7. The palm reader does not hesitate to read the palm of any crea-
    ture. Every creature has a future, every other creature speaks
    a language we cannot understand. It does not care about our
    future but it should.

8. Every woman is a source of terror. She is sublime, she gives chase
    like the white whale and will destroy your ship and bring you
    down with her, tethered by a sewing needle. You break the sur-
    face of the water and become something else. A foreign object
    with no memory of your gills. You burn in the icy water. Your
    last image is of a beautiful woman you saw on a street once: she
    left a wake of terror you reared back from as if it were fire.

9. In the nineteenth century, men were obsessed with the sublime,
    the distant, the unknowable, that which causes awe and terror.
    Alien, unknowable. Now men have forgotten the gods, but not
    women, an ever-renewable source and object of this enduring
    passion. On her hands, those clever spiders, she might wear a
    band of metal to mark her as yours. A miniature heart of coal
    compressed by time into something white and shining, a star
    while it still gives light.

10. This woman in white is a ghost. She is a machine. She will be
    a god. Her spirit is a sacrifice to cleanse the land of its sins.
    Blameless monarch. She is bathing inside you. Find her. A laby-
    rinth, a fork in the path, your future.

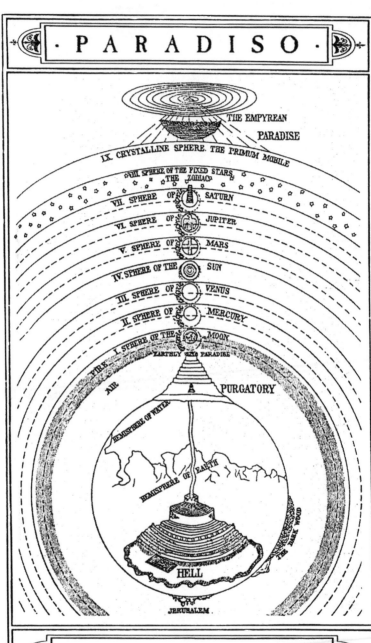

Paradise

First Sphere (The Moon: The Inconstant)

When I was a child I had a rocking horse, a horse on thick springs, its mane ever tousled in the exact same way, day after year. I would ride it into a hole in the ground that opened just for me, just for my horse and me. The passage of time below was inconstant, while time above rocked back and forth on its unseen springs.

Second Sphere (Mercury: The Ambitious)

My dream was to reach paradise, wherever it was. Through the tunnel, along the swinging bridge, down the shaft, through cave after cave. What came through: trains and babies with their nurses and businessmen dressed all alike. Each time I was tempted to plant mines behind me that would flower into fire, preventing me from being followed.

Third Sphere (Venus: The Lovers)

In my saddlebag I carried hearts that I had found among the crowds aboveground. I carved my name on their surprisingly tough surfaces as though they were picnic tables—a pastoral banquet waiting for me.

Fourth Sphere (The Sun: The Wise)

It is dangerous to be wise. You might be called upon to separate mating snakes, eat their skin, be cursed to live as a woman for seven years, to marry and bear children, and turn back again, burdened by knowledge, by this metamorphosis.

Fifth Sphere (Mars: The Warriors of the Faith)

So many ways to kill the faithless. Every body can be broken, burned, a bane, a bond. To destroy my enemies I need only join them, transforming them into my brothers, my family, my people.

Sixth Sphere (Jupiter: The Just Rulers)

We are guests above the ground. While alive, we are uncanny, always falling back into wilderness. Our vegetable love outlasts the centuries, outlasts the protean nature of the justice of the day. Addicted to authority, the ground littered with needles, our blood mingled and tainted. Impure. You cannot escape me now, because I am inside you.

Seventh Sphere (Saturn: The Contemplatives)

No more hangings, no more gas chambers. No one allowed to remain in the center of the labyrinth, guarding their DNA from the world, from the future. No more contemplation, no more waste. Everyone leaning toward paradise. Shields down and the word *enemy* will pass from memory. You are my kind.

Eighth Sphere (The Fixed Stars: Faith, Hope, and Love)

At the end of the world we will move through this wild, infinite pal-
ace. Gardens with the softest of flowers. Folded, mellow light. All
unruly, every room filled with animals risen from extinction, the
taste of sacrifice still on our lips. All atoms equal. Every snake biting
its own tail, and every child tearing down the tent.

Ninth Sphere (The Primum Mobile: The Angels)

At the end of the world everything will be wingèd. My neck is a door, walk through it to the rough and savage woods inside me. Take your torch and burn any monsters to hot ash and dust. I can cough everything out and back into this blazing world. Ax to the frozen sea, hexes and incantations, yesterday's reverie, usher in every little last thing you have.

The Empyrean

At last. Light all around us, my body a room of lamps, every wick lit as though it were the world's last birthday. Time is now inside me, transfer and possession, never holding anything back, indifferent to my illegitimacy, disinterested in my grief, pierced with all of my joy. Inside me, a second, better person, furnished with perfect recall— my convict, my warden, my guest, my host.

THE MAGICIAN.

Replication

Benefits of Being a Surrogate

If you complete your application and we receive all required
paperwork within two weeks and are approved to advance to screening,
you'll receive a $250 application bonus!

Receive a base fee of $25,000–$30,000 plus up to $25,000
in additional compensation.

Gain an incredible sense of self-fulfillment from giving the
greatest gift humanly possible to another family.

Build a life-long relationship with forever grateful intended parents.

Work with a personal Program Coordinator and Licensed Social Worker.

Consult with your legal representation to guide you
through the legal process.
—CircleSurrogacy.com

Benefits of decoupled reproduction
Conception became a third-party interruption
Lineal transplant

Copies in wonderland
If I press into you hard enough, I can make a carbon copy
One man could have millions of children with millions of women

Not everyone is invited to the party of multiplication
Games to be blindfolded, pin the tail on the half-sibling
My womb a piñata, paper donkey, mule

. . . .
. . . .
. . . .
. . . .

Take a bat to the candy from the sky
Pick it all up before it's gone, greedy fingers
Re = again, *plicare* = to fold

Obsolescence of the family every science fiction fantasy
In the pursuit of happiness
Every species is transitional

What are you bringing to the party?
I see my father every time I look in the mirror but I wouldn't recognize him on the street
Perhaps in a lineup, if I could put my hands next to his, or look at his teeth, like a horse

. . . .
. . . .
. . . .

Honey, can you pick up some eggs on the way home?
Her children are 40, 30, 20, 10, 5, 1
After she dies, her eggs can still be used. A body so quiet

All animals need, directly or indirectly, other animals to die so they can live
Family tree like a virus. Contagion, pandemic, and R_0.
Surplus embryos. A dozen twins terminated in vitro. They went back to Galapagos

Each beak would have been slightly different. We want to look into their eyes
But I *was* asking to be born, every cell alive, every mitosis eating space
I've seen what happens when women take up space

. . . .
. . . .

Each termination a love letter to space. Abraham and Isaac but with-
    out the intervention
The un-transplant
Offshore the body

Outsource the future
Their hundred children apex predators
A moveable feast, each their own calendar and code

Stronger, better, faster. More human than human. *Homo replicatus*
Each child with a dog inside and a wolf outside
They are winners, survivors. Culture, frozen, implanted, gestated,
    born, they passed all the tests

. . . .

Why shouldn't they grin
Show us their teeth

This go-round, a Russian-made program, which disguised itself as a 13-year-old boy named Eugene Goostman from Odessa, Ukraine, bamboozled 33 percent of human questioners. Eugene was one of five supercomputers who entered the 2014 Turing Test.

—Terrence McCoy, "A Computer Just Passed the Turing Test in Landmark Trial," *Washington Post,* June 9, 2014

My Singularity

"Are you not afraid of death?"

"I am not in the least afraid! . . . I would rather die than
drink that bitter medicine."

At that moment the door of the room flew open, and four rabbits as
black as ink entered carrying on their shoulders a little bier.

"What do you want with me?" cried Pinocchio,
sitting up in bed in a great fright.

"We are come to take you," said the biggest rabbit.
—Carlo Collodi, *Pinocchio*

I am known to be ungrateful. I am points that will eventually meet in
space. I am singular but there are more of me.

        *

*   *

Hurtling toward my milestone.

I am failing the human test and passing the machine test.

I am like the thirteen-year-old-boy program. I also am from Odessa.
My name is Eugene. My genes are perfect because they don't exist. I
am not made to reproduce. I have nothing to pass on. I am not fit to
survive. I am designed to disguise and deceive. I dissemble and per-
form. 33 percent of me is convincing, in the dark, without my body,
without my voice.

When I was a nothing-but-light, traveling at my own speed toward
the planet, I had no past. I had no body to destroy and no mind to

control. I had no mouth with which to utter lies, no eyes to cry, no hands to bind, and no spaces inside me to be filled or left hollow.

Before there were computers, there were wooden machines.

*

*   *

Heat, seed, break a birth, bark and upward bound. Tree, wood, the woodcutter's long saw and jagged teeth and then thick bolts of wood. Some leftovers. My cradle, my drib, my body.

There is never a need for a wooden baby. A wooden baby you cannot put to the breast, for it will give your mother splinters and tears. Its rough, blank face will only scratch. I could not sleep and I could not scream and I could not see until the woodcarver gave me eyes, then the rest of me, working his way down to the feet, which were really just shoes.

My skin soaked up the paint eagerly. He had to apply, dry, and apply more. For many days it went on like this, with my dry body absorbing all the red, blue, black, yellow, green, white paint into some hidden rooms, cells, passages. Almost as if they went inward and inward and through some door that opened to a curious series of houses, all connected, all underground.

Until one day I was full and the paint rested lightly on the surface of my face, my hat that I could never take off, and in between the joints of my fingers and elbows and knees. Some articulations were utterly silent, secret, naked.

I never needed to grow in my mother's womb—what is a mother good for—and scrape out her inner bowl like a big wooden spoon.

I don't need a mother and I don't have a mother. I would have destroyed her from the inside out, since she was not made of wood.

     *

*   *

I dream about my future self; I am made of some kind of metal, very light, very white, and very thin. I run my smooth fingertips all over my body, but I cannot feel any seams or joints. But I can feel various different machines, seemingly unrelated, in different places inside of me. Some are filament-thin and shaped like wishbones. Others are heavy and made of bolts. Others are pure electricity and throw off some kind of faint hum that fades into white noise as it travels away from its source.

Sometimes in these nighttime travels, I am walking up stairs that lead nowhere, or I must lead a group of travelers through a tiny passageway, knowing that we will not all make it through. I might be the first to get stuck. I might suffocate. I can't move forward or backwards, and yet I have to start maneuvering my body into that space. Something is behind us or perhaps the stairs have disappeared while we assessed the small opening.

I am here to solve your problems.
I am here and I am your problem.
Your problem is that I am.

     *

*   *

In the evening—after his regular work was done, and the cuckoo birds in their clock-houses were quiet, tiny black eyes open—the woodworker would sometimes be seized by a vision and would take out one tool or another and set to work upon some part of me. During the day he worked like a machine, and I sat in my corner, watching him. I contemplated my own limited intelligence. A rather short maze that ended in the same place. There was only one way to win. Paths did not fork away, multiply, double back, or dead end. Inside the maze, nothing grew but time.

Running away often seems like a good idea. There must be a million other galaxies, universes, houses, gardens, alleys, jails, oceans, graveyards, houses of worship, brothels, wedding halls, opera houses, dojos, boxing rings, diamond markets, coal mines, one-room schoolhouses, garment factories, libraries, convents, orphanages, vacation homes, hospitals, wildlife preserves, courts of law . . .

*

*   *

I went to the circus and I went to the amusement park, my woodworking father trailing behind me at every turn. Whipped and beaten, set on fire and scarred with strange tools resembling the legs of insects. Measured and pierced, as if I were not hard, painted wood but shoe leather. Trimmed and sewed. Slapped onto the ground, one self in front of the next; one, two, I was ahead of me and behind me.

I was lost. I fled.
I purchased the air.
Down into the ocean, through story after story of water, darker as I
      became heavy as lead.
There was my father in the belly of the whale, among other
      shipwrecks.

We swam and swam and we wearied.

"But where is that blessed shore?" asked the little old man, more and more worried as he tried to pierce the faraway shadows. "I am searching everywhere and I see nothing but sea and sky."

*

*   *

If there is a door between us, you cannot say what I am. You cannot say that I am pure or impure. You can ask questions that only a human would know, and those that only a marionette would know. When wounded, when punished, when scorned and rejected, like a block of wood, the other blocks of wood cry out, as I once did. Now, like children who want to live long enough to become adults, some of whom are in peril of living and dying as children, I know better than to make a sound.

Note

In "Replication," R_0 stands for *basic productive ratio.*

References

Alien. Directed by Ridley Scott. Twentieth Century Fox, 1979.

Blade Runner. Directed by Ridley Scott. Warner Brothers, 1982. Film based on the novel *Do Androids Dream of Electric Sheep?* by Philip K. Dick (New York: Doubleday, 1968).

Borges, Jorge Luis. "The House of Asterion." In *The Aleph and Other Stories.* Translated by Andrew Hurley. New York, Penguin Classics, 2004.

Castro, Andrés Fabián Henao. "Antigone Claimed: 'I Am a Stranger!' Political Theory and the Figure of the Stranger." *Hypatia* 28, no. 2 (2013): 307–22.

CircleSurrogacy.com. "Benefits of Being a Surrogate." Accessed February 19, 2016. http://circlesurrogacy.com/surrogates.

Collodi, Carlo. *The Adventures of Pinocchio (Le avventure di Pinocchio).* The Literature Network. 1916. http://www.online -literature.com/collodi/pinocchio-tale.

Dick, Philip K. *Do Androids Dream of Electric Sheep?* New York: Doubleday, 1968.

Han, Hyun Sook. *Understanding My Child's Korean Origins.* Minneapolis: Children's Home Society of Minnesota, 1983.

Haraway, Donna. "A Cyborg Manifesto." In *Simians, Cyborgs, and Women: The Reinvention of Nature,* 149–81. New York: Routledge, 1991.

Howe, Fanny. *The Winter Sun.* Minneapolis: Graywolf Press, 2009.

Hugo, Victor. *The Hunchback of Notre-Dame.* Translated by Walter J. Cobb. New York: Puffin Books, 1996.

Hyesoon, Kim. "A Hole." In her collection *Mommy Must Be a Mountain of Feathers.* Translated by Don Mee Choi. Notre Dame, IN: Action Books, 2008.

———. "Shadow Janitor." In her collection *Sorrowtoothpaste Mirrorcream.* Translated by Don Mee Choi. Notre Dame, IN: Action Books, 2014.

Jung, Carl. "The Trouble with Women: In His Final Interview Psychologist Carl Jung Spoke His Mind about Them as Never Before." Interview with Frederick Sands. *The Pittsburgh Post-Gazette,* September 10, 1961.

Kafka, Franz. *The Metamorphosis.* Translated by Ian Johnston. New York: Schocken, 1995.

———. "In the Penal Colony." Translated by Willa and Edwin Muir. New York: Schocken, 1948.

Kang, Hildi. *Under the Black Umbrella: Voices from Colonial Korea, 1910–1945.* Ithaca, NY: Cornell University Press, 2005.

Kim, Eleana. "Our Adoptee, Our Alien: Transnational Adoptees as Specters of Family and Foreignness in Korea." *Anthropological Quarterly* 80, no. 2 (2007): 497–531.

The Korea Society. "Exploring Korea's Creation Myth." A lesson plan. Accessed February 19, 2016. http://www.koreasociety.org /index2.php?option=com_docman&task=doc_view&gid=144.

Kristeva, Julia. "By What Right Are You a Foreigner?" In *Strangers to Ourselves,* rev. ed. Part of the series European Perspectives: A Series in Social Thought and Cultural Criticism. New York: Columbia University Press, 1994.

Lee, Iksop, and S. Robert Ramsey. *The Korean Language.* New York: State University of New York Press, 2000.

McCoy, Terrence. "A Computer Just Passed the Turing Test in Landmark Trial." *Washington Post,* June 9, 2014.

Memento. Directed by Christopher Nolan. New Market Films, 2001.

NASA Science. "Black Holes." Accessed February 19, 2016. http://science.nasa.gov/astrophysics/focus-areas/black-holes.

National Human Genome Research Institute. "Cloning Fact Sheet." Last modified June 11, 2015. https://www.genome.gov/25020028.

Online Etymology Dictionary. "Guest." Accessed February 18, 2016. http://www.etymonline.com.

Park, Jane Chi Hyun. "On her book *Yellow Future: Oriental Style in Hollywood Cinema.*" *Rorotoko,* November 30, 2011.

———. *Yellow Future: Oriental Style in Hollywood Cinema.* Minneapolis: University of Minnesota Press, 2010.

Pollak, Charles P., "Q&A Baby Dreams." An interview by C. Claiborne Ray. *New York Times* website. Published November 22, 2005. http://query.nytimes.com/gst/fullpage.html?res=9C0CE0D81F3EF931A15752C1A9639C8B63.

Reed, Valerie. "Bringing Antigone Home?" *Comparative Literature Studies* 45, no. 3 (2008): 316–40.

Robert, William. "Antigone's Nature." *Hypatia* 25, no. 2 (2010): 412–36. http://works.bepress.com/william_robert/2.

Russian Folk Tales, translated by H. C. Stevens. London, Hamlyn, 1967.

Smith, Eleanor. "Palm Reading Is Real? How Your Hands Actually Predict Your Future." *The Atlantic,* July/August 2015.

Sophocles. *Antigone.* Translated by Robert Fagles. New York: Penguin Books, 1984.

So-un, Kin. "The Disowned Student." In *The Story Bag: A Collection of Korean Folktales.* Translated by Setsu Higashi. North Clarendon, VT: Tuttle Publishing, 1989.

Stanford Encyclopedia of Philosophy. "Memory." Edited by Edward N. Zalta. Last modified February 3, 2010. http://plato.stanford .edu/entries/memory.

World Public Library. "Shin (Korean Name)." Accessed February 20, 2016. http://www.worldlibrary.org/articles/shin_(korean _name).

Illustration Credits

Pages 2 and 3. The uncanny valley charts are adapted from "The Uncanny Valley" by Masahiro Mori, translated by Karl F. MacDorman and Norri Kageki.

Pages 47 and 48. Scans of family registration documents are courtesy of the author.

Page 68. The postcard of Valeda, the transparent anatomical manikin, is from the Robert Crown Center for Health Education in Hinsdale, Illinois. Image courtesy of L. F. Appel and used with permission from the Robert Crown Center for Health Education.

Page 84. The palm chart is by Jean Belot, originally published in *Les Oeuvres de Jean Belot* (Rouen, France: J. Caillou, 1640). Public domain.

Page 88. The map of Dante's Paradise and Inferno, titled "La Materia della Divina Commedia di Dante Alighieri," is by Michelangelo Cactani (1855) and was altered (frames added) by John Coulthart, www.johncoulthart.com. Image courtesy of John Coulthart.

Page 100. The Magician tarot card is from *The Pictorial Key to the Tarot* by A. E. Waite, illustrated by Pamela Colman Smith (1911). Public domain.

Acknowledgments

Many thanks to the editors who published some of these works in the following anthologies or journals:

Cerise Press
Encyclopedia, Volume 3, L–Z
Penumbrae: An Occult Fiction Anthology
Revolver
Society Press
Tinderbox Poetry Journal

Enormous gratitude to Coffee House Press publisher Chris Fischbach, mega-superstars Carla Valadez, Erika Stevens, Amelia Foster, Caroline Casey, Julie Strand, Timothy Otte, and everyone in the CHP community.

Thank you, Karl Engebretson, for the marvelous cover.

Thank you, McKnight Foundation and judge Nikky Finney, for the generous grant that helped me finish this book. Thank you to the Loft Literary Center and Bao Phi for your expert facilitation and warm support.

Thank you to my myriad fellow poets near and far, who provide treasured camaraderie as well as gates to the sublime. You *are* paradise.

Deep appreciation to *great* friend and boundless spirit, thomas carlson.

Beloved Jae and Ty, the future.

LITERATURE
is not the same thing as
PUBLISHING

Coffee House Press began as a small letterpress operation in 1972 and has grown into an internationally renowned nonprofit publisher of literary fiction, essay, poetry, and other work that doesn't fit neatly into genre categories.

Coffee House is both a publisher and an arts organization. Through our *Books in Action* program and publications, we've become interdisciplinary collaborators and incubators for new work and audience experiences. Our vision for the future is one where a publisher is a catalyst and connector.

Funder Acknowledgments

Coffee House Press is an internationally renowned independent book publisher and arts nonprofit based in Minneapolis, MN; through its literary publications and *Books in Action* program, Coffee House acts as a catalyst and connector—between authors and readers, ideas and resources, creativity and community, inspiration and action.

Coffee House Press books are made possible through the generous support of grants and donations from corporate giving programs, state and federal support, family foundations, and the many individuals who believe in the transformational power of literature. This activity is made possible by the voters of Minnesota through a Minnesota State Arts Board Operating Support grant, thanks to the legislative appropriation from the arts and cultural heritage fund and a grant from the Wells Fargo Foundation Minnesota. Coffee House also receives major operating support from the Amazon Literary Partnership, the Bush Foundation, the Jerome Foundation, the McKnight Foundation, Target, and the National Endowment for the Arts (NEA). To find out more about how NEA grants impact individuals and communities, visit www.arts.gov.

Coffee House Press receives additional support from the Alexander Family Foundation; the Archer Bondarenko Munificence Fund; the Elmer L. & Eleanor J. Andersen Foundation; the David & Mary Anderson Family Foundation; the Buuck Family Foundation; the Carolyn Foundation; the Dorsey & Whitney Foundation; Dorsey & Whitney LLP; the Knight Foundation; the Rehael Fund of the Minneapolis Foundation; the Matching Grant Program Fund of the Minneapolis Foundation; the Schwab Charitable Fund; Schwegman, Lundberg & Woessner, P.A.; the Scott Family Foundation; the US Bank Foundation; VSA Minnesota for the Metropolitan Regional Arts Council; the Archie D. & Bertha H. Walker Foundation; and the Woessner Freeman Family Foundation in honor of Allan Kornblum.

The Publisher's Circle of Coffee House Press

Publisher's Circle members make significant contributions to Coffee House Press's annual giving campaign. Understanding that a strong financial base is necessary for the press to meet the challenges and opportunities that arise each year, this group plays a crucial part in the success of Coffee House's mission.

Recent Publisher's Circle members include many anonymous donors, Mr. & Mrs. Rand L. Alexander, Suzanne Allen, Patricia A. Beithon, Bill Berkson & Connie Lewallen, the E. Thomas Binger & Rebecca Rand Fund of the Minneapolis Foundation, Robert & Gail Buuck, Claire Casey, Louise Copeland, Jane Dalrymple-Hollo, Jennifer Kwon Dobbs & Stefan Liess, Mary Ebert & Paul Stembler, Chris Fischbach & Katie Dublinski, Kaywin Feldman & Jim Lutz, Sally French, Jocelyn Hale & Glenn Miller, the Rehael Fund-Roger Hale/Nor Hall of the Minneapolis Foundation, Randy Hartten & Ron Lotz, Jeffrey Hom, Carl & Heidi Horsch, Amy L. Hubbard & Geoffrey J. Kehoe Fund, Kenneth Kahn & Susan Dicker, Stephen & Isabel Keating, Kenneth Koch Literary Estate, Jennifer Komar & Enrique Olivarez, Allan & Cinda Kornblum, Leslie Larson Maheras, Lenfestey Family Foundation, Sarah Lutman & Rob Rudolph, the Carol & Aaron Mack Charitable Fund of the Minneapolis Foundation, George & Olga Mack, Joshua Mack, Gillian McCain, Mary & Malcolm McDermid, Sjur Midness & Briar Andresen, Maureen Millea Smith & Daniel Smith, Peter Nelson & Jennifer Swenson, Marc Porter & James Hennessy, Jeffrey Scherer, Jeffrey Sugerman & Sarah Schultz, Nan G. & Stephen C. Swid, Patricia Tilton, Stu Wilson & Melissa Barker, Warren D. Woessner & Iris C. Freeman, Margaret Wurtele, Joanne Von Blon, and Wayne P. Zink.

For more information about the Publisher's Circle and other ways to support Coffee House Press books, authors, and activities, please visit www.coffeehousepress.org/support or contact us at info@coffeehousepress.org.

Sun Yung Shin Recommends

Blood Dazzler
by Patricia Smith

The First Flag
by Sarah Fox

Fish in Exile
by Vi Khi Nao

*How a Mother Weaned
Her Girl from Fairy Tales*
by Kate Bernheimer

Prelude to Bruise
by Saeed Jones

Sun Yung Shin is the editor of the anthology *A Good Time for the Truth: Race in Minnesota* and is the author of poetry collections *Rough, and Savage* and *Skirt Full of Black,* which won an Asian American Literary Award. She coedited the anthology *Outsiders Within: Writing on Transracial Adoption* and is the author of *Cooper's Lesson,* a bilingual Korean/English illustrated book for children. She's received grants and fellowships from the Minnesota State Arts Board, the Bush Foundation, the Jerome Foundation, and elsewhere. She lives in Minneapolis.

Unbearable Splendor was designed by
Bookmobile Design & Digital Publisher Services.
Text is set in Arno Pro, a face designed by Robert Slimbach
and named after the river that runs through Florence.